This book is dedicated to my pastor Dr. Joe Arthur for his continual help and encouragement for me to continue my Biblical studies and to Dr. Steve Harper and all those that teach at the Harvest Baptist Tabernacle Bible School.

2 Timothy 2:15 "Study to shew thyself approved unto God, a workman that needeth not to be ashamed, rightly dividing the word of truth." (KJV)

The Book of Jude

Modern-Day Apostasy

by

Roger L. Bilbrey

© Copyright 2022 – Roger L. Bilbrey
Tree of Life Coaching
ISBN: 978-1-7332018-5-8

Printed in the United States of America
Roger Bilbrey & Associates---Publisher

Edited Version

WWW.TREEOFLIFECOACHING.ORG

The front cover picture was taken from my personal Scofield KJV Bible

TABLE OF CONTENTS

Chapter 1

A Hidden Treasure

When I first began the study of the Book of Jude, I was asked by my Sunday School teacher if I would be willing to teach a lesson.

I prayed about it and thought the Book of Jude would be perfect for teaching just one lesson in a Sunday morning class. My reasoning was the book has one chapter and only twenty-five verses. How hard could that be? Surely, I would be able to finish a book so small on a Sunday morning!

I arrived that Sunday morning prepared to give my quick presentation of the Book of Jude. I was currently enrolled in Bible College under the teaching of my professor Dr. Steve Harper. Under such outstanding leadership, I had complete confidence that I was prepared to deliver the lesson.

Dr. Harper, while teaching class, loves to use big words. So, jokingly, I told the class, "Today will be a theology class mainly on the bibliology of Jude through a homiletical expository method hoping that we might get a glimpse of a typology of Jesus Christ and even some eschatology, but I promise we won't be getting into cosmetology."

Unfortunately, Dr. Harper was ministering at another church that Sunday, so he couldn't enjoy the humor.

Granted, I don't usually talk that way and won't in this book, but the class got a kick out of it, and that's all that matters. And, for the record, please don't judge Dr. Harper

1

for my feeble attempt at writing this book. He can only do so much with someone like me.

To my surprise, I only covered three verses that morning. Had I not hurried through verse three, we wouldn't have gotten that far.

My Sunday School teacher allowed me another Sunday to finish up, and on that Sunday, we only got through verse five. I knew at that moment that the Book of Jude wasn't one you could rush through.

I decided instead of using up more Sunday School time; I would make a CD on the study and give it to the class members. However, the more I studied, the more I found. It was apparent that I would never be able to put all the content on one CD.

Maybe because of the size of the book, most people overlook it. It is not a book that many preachers preach out of, but as you will soon see, it is a book that would do us good to spend considerable time in meditation and study.

The Book of Jude is a hidden treasure full of knowledge, warnings, encouragement, and a challenge to fight for the faith that was not only good for the time it was written but also fits perfectly for us today.

It is almost as if Jude is looking into a crystal ball at the current society of America and the entire world. There is no doubt that the words penned by Jude were inspired by the Holy Spirit and can be used by us today.

It is a true example of how the Word of God is a living Word that can transcend time, space, and culture.

The Book of Jude is one of the only, if not the only, book that is given entirely to the great apostasy and written for the end times. As you study the Book of Jude, I believe you will agree with me that it is no wonder why it is placed right before the Book of Revelation.

Jude's message is one of the most severe in the New Testament. His statements are clearly justified when we read what was happening in the church then and now.

The Book of Jude can be divided into four sections. I. The Greeting and Reasoning for the Writing. II. Exposing of False Teachers in the Church. III. Warnings and Instructions to Christians, and finally, IV. The Benediction.

You will also discover that the Book of Jude and 2nd Peter chapter 2 almost mirror themselves. For this reason, many believe that one author had either shared his thoughts or used the other's writings to write their own letter to the believers. As we go through this study of the Book of Jude, I will bring out some of those similarities as it helps define what the other is saying.

Many scholars say that the Book of Jude was written in 70 A.D. It is hard for me to believe that the writing of this epistle could have come so late because, in 70 A.D., Jerusalem was destroyed. That being the case, you would think that the most pressing thing for Jude to discuss would be Jerusalem's destruction. This alone makes me believe that the book of Jude must have been written sometime before that event.

It is believed that 2nd Peter was written between 62-68 A.D. If that is true, it would be more in line with the timing of Jude, especially since neither of the writers mentions the destruction of Jerusalem.

It should also be noted that around 64 A.D., the Romans came against the church with much propaganda. Sound familiar with what is going on today in our government?

Many Romans believed the church was the reason for the "Great Fire of Rome," which occurred on July 18, 64 A.D. Some believe Nero himself started the fires and blamed it on the church for his own gain. This fire was so intense that it burnt down in just six days, ten out of fourteen districts of Rome.

We also know that during this time frame, many Christians were killed. I know it sounds impossible, but if America continues on her path, it will not surprise me if Christians are killed on our soil because of the lies and hate toward our faith.

I think it would be good to see what was taking place between 64-70 A.D. to get a better insight into the conditions the church was under during this writing.

I have already mentioned the Great Fire in 64 A.D. It was around this same time that Christians began to be persecuted. Nero was a leader during this time. It seemed he had great hatred toward the church and was considered one of the worst in torturing the saints. It was nothing for him to skin alive Christians or set them on fire and hang them on a post for lights.

In 66 A.D., the Roman procurator of Judea, Gessius Florus, killed around 3,600 Jews, most of which were crucified. At that time, Christians began to flee to Judea.

The Jews tried to fight back, which is now known as the Great Revolt. This revolt lasted about four years and ended with hundreds of thousands of lost lives.

We learned most of what we know about this revolt from Josephus, a Roman-Jewish scholar. Josephus also fought in the revolt against the Romans. He was eventually kept as a slave and interpreter. Then later, he was freed and granted Roman citizenship.

Also, during the year of 66 A.D., the Jews fought with each other. This was due to three different fractions claiming to have as their leader the "Messiah." And, to top it off, there were many earthquakes reported during that time frame.

In 67 A.D., four thousand Roman soldiers enter Judea to destroy the Jewish revolt. By 70 A.D., the Temple and Jerusalem were destroyed. According to Josephus, the death toll came to 1,197,000. The remaining Jews were sold into slavery.

Two of the church's prominent leaders, Peter and Paul, were executed between 64-68 A.D. Can you understand why there was so much happening in the church during this time?

Although the Book of Jude is considered part of our canon, it was not widely accepted by many. It was disputed as well as other books we have in our Bible, such as Hebrews, Revelation, 1st Peter, 2nd and 3rd John, and James.

There were several reasons why these writings were disputed. First, for the Jews, the statements of being justified by faith and not of works didn't settle well with them. As most know, the Jews were instructed to obey the Law God had given them in the Old Testament. We now know that our flesh could never live to the fullness of the Law.

Christ came to set us free from the Law by being the perfect sacrifice needed to satisfy God. Christ brought us GRACE!!! No longer are we bound by the Law. Christ set us free! It is by grace and grace alone that we make it to Heaven.

That being said, I think modern-day Christians feel that they no longer need to strive to live holy, believing that the Law is done away with. But for me, although Christ set us free from the Law, we should still try our best to live holy and pleasing to God. We should try to do it not because we have to but because we love and appreciate what Christ completed work on Calvary did for us.

As Paul clearly pointed out, Christ's grace is not a license to sin. "What shall we say then? Shall we continue in sin, that grace may abound?" Romans 6:1.

Another reason that Jude is disputed is that he quotes from the book of Enoch and The Assumption of Moses. I will go into more detail about this as we get to verse 14 of Jude.

The problem was that during the 2nd Century, the Gnostics were playing a big part in the church, and they were writing letters claiming it was for the church.

As a sample of their false teachings, the Gnostic philosophy denied the biblical doctrine of creation and the incarnation of Christ.

They even contradicted their own beliefs. For instance, they didn't believe that they had to live by a moral law, but at the same time, they accepted abusing the body to obtain more spirituality.

These ideas contradict each other and are certainly against what our Bible teaches. It is believed that although they were mainly present in the 2nd century, their roots were in the church during the time of Jude and possibly even before Christ.

Because of false teaching and many writers claiming to be Christians yet contradicting the Christian belief, many of the books we have in our Bible today had to be looked over carefully to make sure they were from God or not.

Around the 1700s, the Muratorian fragment was discovered by the famous historian Ludovico Antonio Muratori. It is believed to have been written sometime in the 2nd century. Within the manuscript is a list of books that the Roman Church considered authoritative at that time. The Book of Jude is among those listed, and Jude has universally been recognized by 350 AD as authentic.

Not all of the books that we have in our canon made this list. It is interesting to note that even today, books that we have in the New Testament are still being disputed.

One shocking thing to note is that even Martin Luther doubted the canonicity of Hebrews, James, Jude, and the

Apocalypse of John. This was evident in the way he listed them. But, it should be noted that he did place them in his canon.

I believe a true student of the Word of God can be assured that every book and scripture in the Bible today was inspired and meant to be included. Each scripture correlates with the other writers and verifies its authenticity.

Other books that didn't make it into our canon were because of variations or statements that didn't completely go along with the other writings. That is not to say that there wasn't truth in them, but just because they didn't entirely and fully agree with the other books, it wasn't accepted into the canon.

I believe as you study the Book of Jude, you will be able to see that it is a book divinely written, and it not only confirms other writings in the Bible but the events spoken of in those days can be seen as truth today.

I hope you find this book helpful in your study and growth in the Word of God. While reading this study, I pray you will examine yourself to see where you might be lacking in servanthood and walk with the Lord.

"See then that ye walk circumspectly, not as fools, but as wise, Redeeming the time, because the days are evil. Wherefore be ye not unwise, but understanding what the will of the Lord is." Ephesians 5:15-17.

Let's begin our journey into "The Book of Jude."

Chapter 2

To Whom it May Concern

"Jude, the servant of Jesus Christ, and brother of James, to them that are sanctified by God the Father, and preserved in Jesus Christ, and called: Mercy unto you, and peace, and love, be multiplied." Jude verses 1-2.

In the opening of this Epistle, the author leaves the reader with no doubt about who wrote it, *"Jude."* Jude is the English version of his name, and in Greek, it is actually a derivative of Judas, a variant of Judah that means praise.

It could be that Judas was given the name Jude in the English version of the Bible to make sure no one would mistake him for Judas Iscariot, the one who betrayed Jesus Christ.

Although he mentions his name, some still debate who Jude is. Some say it is one of the twelve, while others believe it to be the brother of James and half-brother of Jesus Christ or at least a close cousin.

One thing the author wants us to understand, first and foremost undeniably, is that he is *"the servant of Jesus Christ."* He wants all to know that he belongs to Jesus Christ and has devoted his life to be His servant.

It's evident that Jude is not ashamed to be called a servant of Christ, and he viewed his position as Christ's servant as the highest form of honor. Oh, if only believers today were this proud that we are servants of the Most High.

Instead, many Christians today seem to be ashamed of Christ. You never hear some of them mention His name, much less tell total strangers that they belong to Him. If we as believers could ever once get a glimpse of the majesty of our Lord and Savior, I believe our attitude would change to be more like Jude.

Being a servant is the opposite of what the world would deem something to be proud of. Instead, we are trained to focus on being all we can be.

We measure people by their success in life or their social circles. We hold people like movie stars, athletes, the super-wealthy, and politicians as something to strive to achieve. These people who are regarded so highly will one day lose it all. All their success in life is temporal and, for the most part, will leave no lasting effects. One day, they and everyone else who has ever lived will bow before the King of Kings and Lord of Lords, Jesus Christ.

We send our kids to the best schools. We get them involved in all kinds of activities to broaden their chances in life and push them toward success.

There is nothing wrong with that, provided that we make sure to teach them what is of utmost importance in life. Our concern should be about Jesus Christ, doing what He wants us to do, and teaching our children that only a relationship with Jesus Christ will bring joy and satisfaction in life and give them eternal life. *"He must increase, but I must decrease."* John 3:30.

If they make it to the highest office of President of the United States or become the wealthiest and most influential person on the planet and not have Christ, they have NOTHING! *"For what shall it profit a man, if he shall gain the whole world, and lose his own soul?"* Mark 8:36

To drive this point home, I am reminded of a missionary giving a life lesson he learned.

The missionary had been on the mission field in a third-world country since his boy was just a baby. The area where he missioned had no influential or wealthy people, no television or cell phones, no running water, no heating or air conditioning, just the basics of life.

One day, when they were in the States to gather more support, a large church with many wealthy and well-known people invited the missionary to come and tell his story.

After the service, he was invited to go home with one of the prominent people to a cookout they were having. Many other notable people would be there as well.

The missionary felt out of place. He didn't have fancy clothes, didn't talk like them, and certainly couldn't relate to the high class they lived in. Yet, he felt it necessary to go and maybe get more support for the ministry.

When he arrived, he was overwhelmed by the cookout's abundance. There was so much food, things to do for the children, and many important people.

He felt so out of place. Then to make things worse, he overheard a conversation some of the young boys were having in front of his son.

The young boys were bragging about who they knew. One mentioned that his dad knew the mayor. The boy made sure to point out that the mayor was in control of the whole city.

Another boy spoke up and said, "That's nothing! My dad knows the governor who controls the whole state. "

Each boy tried to top the other on who they knew. The missionary looked at his son, whose head was bowed low. He knew they didn't know anyone that had power and influence. He felt sorry for his son, knowing the embarrassment and humiliation he must have been feeling.

He said he spoke a silent prayer to God, complaining to God about how much they had given up to serve Him. His son had missed out on many opportunities he could have had should they have stayed in the States.

But then he noticed something strange. His son lifted his head, his eyes began to sparkle, and pride overcame his face.

The missionary couldn't imagine what changed his boy's attitude. But then, he heard something come out of his mouth that filled the missionary's heart with pride.

The missionary's son squared his shoulders, looked straight into the other boys' eyes, and said,
"I got you all beat! My dad knows Jesus, and He is over EVERYTHING!"

Oh, how true a statement. If we know Jesus, we know the King of Kings and Lord of Lords, the Creator of the universe! Why should any of us be ashamed of that? What an honor, a privilege, and a social standing to be a part of His royal family!!!

The type of servant that Jude is referring to is a bondservant. A bondservant was a slave at one time, but because they loved their master so much, they willingly gave themselves as servants to them for the rest of their lives. This showed genuine love and loyalty to the master. It is an even more profound form of relationship than being just a family member of the master. As a family member, you can always disown your family. But as a bondservant, your commitment is for a life of belonging to the master.

A person became a slave for many reasons during those days. It was not the same as how most Americans viewed slavery. This type of enslaved person in the days of Jude is still active in certain parts of the world today.

Frequently, you became a slave for a period of time to repay a debt you might have owed. In Rome, there were many slaves who later decided to be bondservants to their masters. It is estimated that 1/3 of the population of Rome during that time were slaves or bondservants.

A bondservant had no rights of his own. They were under total control of the master to do to them as he pleased. Their love and decision to become his bondservant also had to have a tremendous amount of trust that the master would treat them well and fairly.

Jude was not the only one who called himself a bondservant. James, Peter, and Paul also addressed themselves as bondservants of Christ.

In all reality, you are a servant to only one of two rulers, either Jesus Christ or Satan. Romans 6:16, *"Know ye not, that to whom ye yield yourselves servants to obey, his servants ye are to whom ye obey; whether of sin unto death, or of obedience unto righteousness?"*

It is not a shameful thing to be a bondservant of Jesus. The Lord Himself was a willing servant of God. *"For even the Son of man came not to be ministered unto, but to minister, and to give his life a ransom for many."* Mark 10:45. Again, in Philippians 2:6-8, *"Who, being in the form of God, thought it not robbery to be equal with God: But made himself of no reputation, and took upon him the form of a servant, and was made in the likeness of men: And being found in fashion as a man, he humbled himself, and became obedient unto death, even the death of the cross."*

Christ showed himself as an example of what we should be to God. We should be willing to be a bondservant to Him. By doing so, it shows our love, commitment, and trust in Him.

As a bondservant, we shouldn't question God's plan and desire for us. We don't know the end goal He wants to obtain. Since we are bondservants, we really don't have the right to complain when we go through trials. He guides us in life and only has the best intentions for us and others. We must only trust in His decisions.

We might be bondservants to Him, but He has freed us from the bondage of sin, and we live as free people of God! John 8:36 *"If the Son therefore shall make you free, ye shall be free indeed."* Hallelujah, glory to His name!

Jude further identifies himself by stating, *"and brother of James."*

Jude, as well as James, were common names during those times. He didn't detail which James he was talking about; because of this, there is a division as to whom he was referring.

As already mentioned earlier, some believe that the James he was referring to was the James that was part of the twelve disciples.

Although this debate has been going on for hundreds of years, it wouldn't seem probable that it was James of the twelve disciples. One of the reasons is that James (the disciple) was killed by Herod Agrippa around 44 A.D.

If it is James the disciple, we have a problem in Acts 21:18, which happened after James the disciple's death. *"And the day following Paul went in with us unto James; and all the elders were present."* Acts 21:18.

James' death was recorded in Acts 12:1-2. *"Now about that time Herod the king stretched forth his hands to vex certain of the church. And he killed James the brother of John with the sword."* Acts 12:1-2.

Another compelling reason is that at the time Jude wrote this, James, the disciple, was not well known. That being the

15

case, his mentioning his brother's name wouldn't have brought much clarity as to whom he spoke about.

On the contrary, had he been talking about James, the half-brother of Christ, people would have been very familiar with him. Why? Because he was the Bishop of the church located in Jerusalem.

It is further believed that James the Bishop was the half-brother of Christ. Many also believe it was he that was mentioned in Matthew 13:55, *"Is not this the carpenter's son? is not his mother called Mary? and his brethren, James, and Joses, and Simon, and Judas?"*

I want you to notice that in this verse, Jude's name is Judas. Still, there is a debate about whether the people mentioned here were actually half-brothers of Jesus or some type of kin like a cousin since the term brethren was used.

You can also note that if James whose mentioned in Matthew was one of the twelve, then his brother John wasn't mentioned. James and John were brothers and known as "the sons of thunder." Their father was Zebedee.

It is interesting to note that James the disciple didn't have a problem believing that Christ was who He said He was. However, James and Jude didn't think Christ was the Messiah until after the resurrection. John 7:5, *"For neither did his brethren believe in him."* The word brethren here in the original language meant brother or close kin.

In fact, many scholars believe that when Mary, the mother of Jesus, and His brethren came to speak to Him in Matthew chapter 12 and Mark chapter 6, they were actually trying to get Christ out of where he was teaching the people because they feared He was losing His mind.

Don't judge James and Jude too harshly about not believing Christ was the Messiah. Since Christ died on the cross, we who have accepted Christ now are sons and daughters of God. We have the Holy Spirit living inside us, confirming who Christ is. Yet how many times do we doubt that Christ can handle our problems? That Christ has the answers to all of our situations. Do you genuinely believe that after knowing Christ intimately and being part of His family, He will be able to meet all of your needs without question? It's easy to doubt at times. Isn't it?

To me, this is clear that Jude is referring to James, the Bishop of the church at the time. But even in this, there is still division as to who the father was. Some believe they were Joseph's sons, and still, others believe they were sons of Alphaeus. Here is one of those places in the Bible where there is not enough information to give a dogmatic opinion. All we know for sure is that Jude had a brother named James, whom most people of that time should have known.

But, if that Jude is the half-brother of Jesus, isn't it amazing how he didn't mention that first? He could have boasted of being related to God's very own Son or at least close kin to Him. But instead, he first said he was a servant to Christ and then mentioned his brother next.

I believe he didn't mention he was kin to Jesus because he didn't want any praise or honor that would have come from that, but rather all the attention would go directly to Christ.

I don't know about you, but most people, me included, love to brag about who we are related to, especially if that person is well known. Can you imagine yourself being a sibling of Christ? How would you address that to others? The answer to that question might make us check our heart to ensure it isn't full of pride or a desire to be noticed.

Now Jude tells whom he is addressing, *"to them that are sanctified by God the Father."* The word sanctified means to make holy, consecrated, or set apart. So Jude is obviously talking to those who have accepted the Lord Jesus Christ as their Savior.

First, I want you to notice a crucial two-letter word, "by." We are sanctified "by" God the Father, not our own works or doing. Paul makes it undeniable that we in ourselves could never make our flesh holy. Romans 8:7-8 *"Because the carnal mind is enmity against God: for it is not subject to the law of God, neither indeed can be. So then they that are in the flesh cannot please God."*

I know people who genuinely believe that they live a holy life. If that be the case, there was no need for Christ to come and die for our sins. They use scriptures like, *"But as he which hath called you is holy, so be ye holy in all manner of conversation;"* 1st Peter 1:15 or *"Sanctify yourselves therefore, and be ye holy: for I am the Lord your God."* Leviticus 20:7.

When we read verses like the one above, it does appear that we can be holy if we work hard enough. But how can we explain what Paul said about the flesh never can please God?

To understand better, we need to see the steps to sanctification. The first stage of sanctification is when a person surrenders to the Lord Jesus Christ. He, at that moment, is immediately set apart for God and made holy by His working through His Son, Jesus Christ. This is a "positional sanctification." This is a permanent, once-for-all act. Christ's blood paid for our sin debt. When God looks at us, He does so through the perfect, holy, unblemished blood of Christ. Because of our position with Christ, we have been made holy. We have been set aside.

But that does not free us to live any way we please. The second part of sanctification is what could be called "progressive sanctification." With this part, a believer determines within himself to discipline his life by yielding to the Holy Spirit for help to live a holy life as much as possible daily. This part of sanctification will continue for as long as the believer lives on earth. It should be something we strive for because of the love we have for Christ and appreciation for Him paying our debt.

The only way that we can come close to being more holy is through daily Bible reading and prayer. The Bible states, *"Thy word have I hid in mine heart, that I might not sin against thee."* Psalm 119:11. Reading God's Word daily will give us strength and encouragement and shed light on where we are missing the mark.

Ephesians 5:26-27 shows us the cleansing power of the Word. *"That he might sanctify and cleanse it with the washing of water by the word, That he might present it to himself a glorious church, not having spot, or wrinkle, or any such thing; but that it should be holy and without blemish."*

Brothers and sisters in Christ, we **ARE** the church, and He uses His Word to cleanse and sanctify us. So it is imperative for us to have the Word of God in us by reading and meditating on it.

Finally, praise God, there is "eternal sanctification." That is when the believer, either through death or the rapture, we will be with God eternally, forever to be without sin and set apart to God and His service. That is when we will be totally, entirely, and completely sanctified and holy, and it is done all by God!

1st Peter 1:2 explains it a little better, *"Elect according to the foreknowledge of God the Father, **through sanctification of the Spirit, unto obedience and sprinkling of the blood of Jesus Christ**: Grace unto you, and peace, be multiplied."* and further in 1st Peter 2:3, *"**According as his divine power hath given unto us all things that pertain unto life and godliness, through the knowledge of him** that hath called us to glory and virtue..."*

Jesus told Peter, James, and John in the garden that prayer would help keep us from temptation. *"Watch and pray, that ye enter not into temptation: the spirit indeed is willing, but the flesh is weak."* Matthew 26:41.

The Word of God and prayer are so important that they are listed in the whole armor of God that we use to fight the enemy of our faith. I believe if it is listed in your warfare armor, it is essential to winning the fight.

There is one other important detail I want to mention before going further. In the original Hebrew, the verse reads "Father God," not "God the Father." When you read it in the original, it takes on a whole different meaning. By saying "Father God," it takes on the intimacy of a father and a child, and not just a God or Father to everyone on earth. God wants us to know that we are His children. Especially in the New Testament, where both Jew and Gentile are made sons and daughters through Jesus Christ our Lord.

Jude goes on to say that the people he is talking about are *preserved in Jesus Christ.* The word preserved here refers to keeping an eye upon or protecting from harm.

From the moment a person accepts Christ into their life, they become a target of Satan. Satan is not so much concerned with the believer himself as he is out to hurt Christ by attacking one of His children.

Paul warns us that we are fighting against evil spirits whose job is to destroy our joy, testimony, and, yes, even our lives if they could. Satan knows that a believer that is indeed sold out for the working of Christ could bring havoc on his plans.

It is so comforting to know that Christ is keeping a watchful eye on those He loves. His Spirit is also here to give us strength when we are weak and guidance when we can't find our way. Being preserved in Christ Jesus shows that God will be there for us in the past, present, and future.

But how much more can we rejoice to know that there is nothing the enemy can do to keep us from going to Heaven and being with our Lord? We are sealed, preserved, kept, unto the day of redemption through Christ Jesus!" *"And I give unto them eternal life; and they shall never perish, neither shall any man pluck them out of my hand."* John 10:28.

Finally, Jude says, *"and called."* Some believe that Jude is referring to only the messianic Jews. However, 1st Corinthians 1:24 makes it very plain who the called are. *"But unto them which are called, both Jews and Greeks, Christ the power of God, and the wisdom of God."*

To me, the called can only be those who have yielded to the Holy Spirit's call to salvation, both Jews and Greek, bond and free. In other words, the Church of the living God.

Notice in verse one we have the working of the Father, the Son, and the Holy Ghost. God helps keep us sanctified, Christ keeps us protected, and the Holy Spirit calls us to salvation and leads us.

In verse two, Jude tells what he desires for us all to have, *"Mercy unto you, and peace, and love, be multiplied."*

It is fitting that he listed mercy first, for without that, none of us would have any hope. Then, as it is today, there was an abundance of sin. We in America have for a long time been existing because of the mercy of God. But our nation isn't the only thing that God's mercy has spared; we personally have been too. The Bible says that we **all** have sinned and come short of the glory of God. If it were not for the mercy of God, we would at this moment be in hell.

Mercy is active compassion for mankind. Mercy is the act of not administering justice when justice is due. God's mercy is entirely a lifeline given by the Heavenly Father to reconcile us back to Him. Titus 3:5 states, *"Not by works of righteousness which we have done, but according to his mercy he saved us, by the washing of regeneration, and renewing of the Holy Ghost;"* Aren't you glad for the mercy of God?

It is through the mercy of God that we can have peace.

Peace with God - When mankind sinned in the garden, it caused enmity between God and us. God despises sin and has a divine hatred toward it. But through the gift of salvation by Christ His Son, we have peace with God. Romans 5:1; *"Therefore being justified by faith, we have peace with God through our Lord Jesus Christ..."*

Peace within ourselves - It is a peace that we can have when everything is going wrong. *"Peace I leave with you, my peace I give unto you: not as the world giveth, give I unto you. Let not your heart be troubled, neither let it be afraid."* John 14:27. *"I will both lay me down in peace, and sleep: for thou, Lord, only makest me dwell in safety."* Psalms 4:8.

Peace with one another - Proverbs 16:7, *"When a man's ways please the Lord, he maketh even his enemies to be at peace with him."*

Peace of mind - Isaiah 26:3, *"Thou wilt keep him in perfect peace, whose mind is stayed on thee: because he trusteth in thee."*

Jude further wishes for his readers *"love."* The type of love mentioned in this verse is "agape" love. It is the same type of love that God gave to mankind when the Bible stated in John 3:16, *"For God so loved the world..."*

It is love toward God and toward man. Christ let us know the importance of this kind of love. Matthew 22:37-40, *"Jesus said unto him, Thou shalt love the Lord thy God with all thy heart, and with all thy soul, and with all thy mind. This is the first and great commandment. And the second is like unto it, Thou shalt love thy neighbour as thyself. On these two commandments hang all the law and the prophets."*

Christ gives us a guideline to see if we have true love toward God. 1st John 4:20, *"If a man say, I love God, and hateth his brother, he is a liar: for he that loveth not his brother whom he hath seen, how can he love God whom he hath not seen?"*

Many people give excuses for why they don't love someone. They may bring up something that person had done to them in the past, or I've heard time and time again when a couple splits that they have "fallen out of love."

These are man's feeble attempts not to obey what God tells us to do. God never asks us to do anything He is unwilling to do Himself. And He has shown us without a doubt that we should love people no matter what. He did it with the love He had for us when we didn't deserve it. *"But God commendeth his love toward us, in that, while we were yet sinners, Christ died for us."* Romans 5:8.

If God loved us so much when we were miserable, disgusting, unworthy sinners, how can we justify not loving people who don't live up to our expectations? It is not a request from God that we love one another; **IT IS A COMMANDMENT.**

Jude completes this verse by adding, *"be multiplied."* The word multiplied is singular here. It only relates to love. He not only wants us to have mercy and peace but love. He wants love to be abundant and increasing in our daily lives.

The only way we can have love multiplied in our lives is through God's mercy and by us being in His will. It is love from God, love for God, and love for one another increasing daily. Is it happening in your life? If not, check up to see why it isn't.

Chapter 3

A Change of Heart

"Beloved, when I gave all diligence to write unto you of the common salvation, it was needful for me to write unto you, and exhort you that ye should earnestly contend for the faith which was once delivered unto the saints." Jude verse 3.

It is to be noted that verse three is one of the key verses in the book of Jude. Jude starts verse three with the intimate term *"beloved."* Most commentaries have overlooked the power of this little word and the importance of why Jude included it in his opening. Jude is showing that the people he addresses are more than acquaintances. These are people dear to his heart.

King Solomon and Daniel are a couple of people in the Bible who state that we were **beloved** of God. In his love for his female companion, Solomon wrote the Song of Solomon, which is dedicated to whom he repeatedly calls his **beloved**. Many of the apostles also addressed the people they wrote to as their **beloved**. Several times in the Scriptures, God spoke audibly and said of Christ, *"This is my **beloved** Son."*

When a person has a deep love for someone, they are exceptionally watchful and protective over them, and their well-being is at the top of their mind. We are Christ's beloved; that is why He has a watchful eye over us. We mean so much to His heart that He not only died for us but showed He was careful about whom He sent to watch after us. This was proven when He questioned Peter's love for Him three times before He told Peter to feed His sheep. By the way, the love Peter said he had boiled down to a brotherly type of love. Christ desires us to have a more intimate love for Him than a brotherly type.

It was out of this love that Jude not only wrote this letter but made it a top priority to get it to them quickly.

As fellow believers of Jesus Christ, we should hold all those in the faith as our beloved and be watchful and ready to help at any given time as if they were our immediate family and most precious beloved. *"And walk in love, as Christ also hath loved us, and hath given himself for us an offering and a sacrifice to God for a sweet smelling savour."* Ephesians 5:2.

Jude goes on to explain his original intent for the letter, *"when I gave all diligence to write unto you of the common salvation..."*

The word diligence in Greek means overcoming zeal, eagerness, or to hasten. In this case, it was for the subject he was going to write about, "the common salvation."

"Common salvation" is a term that is not found anywhere else in the Scripture. The word common should not be confused with the definition that is in our language, which means *"done often or done by more than one."* But instead, the description of something that is shared by all. It refers to the salvation that the Jews and Gentiles now share through Jesus Christ.

When we look back, we can understand why Jude wanted to get his message out about this salvation as soon as possible. We today understand the salvation that Christ brought so much better than the Jews did in Jude's day because we have the New Testament.

Because of the topic of this common salvation Jude wanted to write about, many believe he was writing strictly to the Jews. As we go further, you will be able to understand why. But I still feel that he was writing to both Jews and Gentiles because of the things he eventually felt more important to address.

In Jude's day, as in the days of Peter and Paul, most Christian Jews were opposed to converting Gentiles to the Christian faith. Most of it developed because of the practices the Jews had to observe under the Law that God gave them.

We know by the Word of God that Peter opposed the idea until God sent him a vision to understand better what Christ had done on Calvary to bring both Jews and Gentiles into the faith and right standing with God. Read Acts chapter 10.

Peter and many other Christian Jews felt the only way a Gentile could have salvation was by the Gentile keeping the Mosaic Law and being circumcised. Paul called Peter and the other Christian Jews out on this, as we find in Galatians chapter 2.

But even Paul, before being converted, was against the Christians and felt he was right doing so because of his former religious upbringing. I think it is worth the time to read Philippians 3:4-6 to understand why he felt that way. *"Though I might also have confidence in the flesh. If any other man thinketh that he hath whereof he might trust in the flesh, I more: Circumcised the eighth day, of the stock of Israel, of the tribe of Benjamin, an Hebrew of the Hebrews; as touching the law, a Pharisee; Concerning zeal, persecuting the church; touching the righteousness which is in the law, blameless."*

Paul was trying to let them know, if works could make it, he surely would. But we now know that the Law was weak, and our flesh could never hold up to it. Paul, in verse 9 of Philippians chapter 3, lets them know it's not by his works, *"And be found in him, not having mine own righteousness, which is of the law, but that which is through the faith of Christ, the righteousness which is of God by faith..."*

Many Christian Jews had a problem with this teaching because they had been living under the Law for thousands of years. Even Christ, before He was crucified, observed the Jewish Law. A few times, He strayed from what they said the Law stated, like when He plucked corn or when He healed people on the Sabbath, but that was to show the Jews two things. One was that they were adding to the Law man-made traditions because Deuteronomy 23:25 plainly taught that you could pluck corn while going through a field on the Sabbath. He also wanted to show that He was the giver of the Law and it was okay to do good on the Sabbath. *" And he said unto them, The sabbath was made for man, and not man for the sabbath: Therefore the Son of man is Lord also of the sabbath."* Mark 2:27-28. The Sabbath was made for man's benefit so he could rest and for the physical benefits of that rest.

But where the Law was weak in bringing salvation, Christ came to deliver us from the Law. Throughout His ministry, He taught that men would have to believe in Him. John 6:29 is one of those examples, *"Jesus answered and said unto them, This is the work of God, that ye believe on him whom he hath sent."* And, in the verse that almost every believer can quote, Christ shows that this common salvation is open to all. John 3:16, *"For God so loved the world, that he gave his only begotten Son, that **whosoever** believeth in him should not perish, but have everlasting life."*

After Paul was converted, he was one of the most influential people to explain that salvation is by faith and faith alone in Christ Jesus. It is not by any work that we can do but rather the completed work that Christ did on Calvary and His resurrection.

The Great Commission should not only settle that this common salvation is available to all but that we should deliver it to all. *"And he, (speaking of Christ) said unto them, Go ye into all the world, and preach the gospel to every creature. He that believeth and is baptized shall be saved; but he that believeth not shall be damned."* Mark 16: 15-16.

Before going on, I would like to add that Christ is not only the shared salvation, but it's only one salvation; it's the only way to Heaven. Acts 4:12, *"Neither is there salvation in any other: for there is none other name under heaven given among men, whereby we must be saved."* John 10:1, *"Verily, verily, I say unto you, He that entereth not by the door into the sheepfold, but climbeth up some other way, the same is a thief and a robber."* It doesn't matter what Oprah or anyone else says; the only way to God is through His Son, Jesus Christ!

But as necessary as it was to talk about the common salvation and make sure his readers knew the truth, Jude felt there was a more pressing issue to address. He said, *"...it was needful for me to write unto you and exhort you..."* That statement meant that the subject he was going to talk about needed to be discussed immediately. And not to some of them, but all needed to heed and listen. The implications were too significant to delay letting them know. Jude saw the evil that was coming into the church.

And what was so pressing? *"...that ye should earnestly contend for the faith..."* The word contend was a strong word. It derives from a military term that means to prepare for war. Jude is warning the church to defend the faith in an age of apostasy. What he saw coming into the church to destroy it was worth fighting at all costs, even to the point of torture, prison, or worse, death.

As Christians, we are in a battle but not of flesh and blood. We are in a battle with the enemy in the spirit realm. A battle for our faith. A battle for our morals. And yes, now, even a battle for our country.

The problem with our churches today is we have far too long allowed things to go on and not taken a stand against them for fear of being called bigot, hater, homophobic, and the like.

We have an obligation to God to let the people know God's rules and standards and the way to salvation. To do less is a disservice to God.

The word contend also compared to the struggles the Grecian athletes would go through before and during an event. Paul used the analogy of being a fighter, a runner, and a soldier in 2nd Timothy 4:7. We must stand against evil and evil practices but do so in love, not in a hateful manner.

When looking over Jerusalem and its sinful condition, Christ didn't speak harshly but instead said He would take them under his wings if they just allowed Him to do so.

He spoke with compassion on the cross when He said, *"...forgive them for they know not what they do."* The act of sin should cause us anger, but that anger should never be directed toward the sinner but the cause, which is Satan.

We must live a holy life as much as possible by example and gently warn them of their sins. Instead of anger, it should bring us such compassion that our hearts break for them because we know it is through ignorance they do what they do. We should know that Satan has them blinded and leading them to a road of eternal damnation.

We need to remember that, but by the grace of God, there go I. We should thank God every day for sending someone to us to show us the truth and for the Holy Spirit that guided us toward salvation.

Out of love, may we also contend and fight for what we believe. Let's do our part to witness and lead others to Christ. Let's fight the true enemy of the church, Satan, and his followers' spirit.

And what faith are we fighting for? The faith *"which was once delivered unto the saints."*

This faith was a once and for all faith. This faith needs no changes, additions, or subtractions. It is a faith that is able to endure all by itself for the rest of eternity. It is a faith that settled the enmity between God and man. It was a complete faith. It was an accepted faith. It was a divine faith. It was a conquering faith. It was a delivering faith. It was non-other than the promised faith fulfilled by our Lord and Savior Jesus Christ with His death, burial, and resurrection, the faith in the blood of Christ to cover our sins. And it is attainable by simple trust in Him and His complete, once and for all work.

The faith in the Gospel of Jesus Christ was and is sufficient once it was brought to mankind. It will work in every generation and time frame. Hebrews 13:8 says, *"Jesus Christ the same yesterday, and to day, and for ever."* And this faith is for all, *"There is neither Jew nor Greek, there is neither bond nor free, there is neither male nor female: for ye are **all** one in Christ Jesus."* Galatians 3:28.

When Christ said on the cross, "It is finished," the battle was won at that moment. It was the one and only way to be reconciled to God. It provided us the privilege to come before the throne of God and make our requests and petitions known. It provided a place of safety and a place to go in a time of trouble. It brought us into a relationship with God by becoming adopted into His family.

Chapter 4

Unwanted Guest

"For there are certain men crept in unawares, who were before of old ordained to this condemnation, ungodly men, turning the grace of our God into lasciviousness, and denying the only Lord God, and our Lord Jesus Christ."
Jude verse 4.

Starting in this verse and on, Jude explains why we must contend for the faith and begins to expose false teachers and their teaching. He also points out how the believers can contend for the faith and finish strong.

He is most concerned because this is not something that may happen in the future; it was happening inside the church as he was writing this letter, *"For there are certain men **crept in unawares**..."* These people were already within the church assembly, and worse, they sneaked in without anyone in the church noticing.

How could this happen? In 2nd Timothy 3:4-5, Paul warned the church and gave examples of what to look for to prevent this from happening. Paul mentions their characteristics, *"Traitors, heady, highminded, lovers of pleasures more than lovers of God; Having a form of godliness, but denying the power thereof: from such turn away. For of this sort are they which creep into houses, and lead captive silly women laden with sins, led away with divers lusts."*

However, Jude may not have had the luxury of reading what Paul wrote. But, by what Paul wrote, he must have witnessed some of the things Jude mentioned for himself.

But even knowing what to look for, these false teachers still infiltrate some of today's most sound doctrinal and sanctified churches. They creep in; they don't come in all boisterous and against everything we believe. They come in first, smelling like us, talking like us, and acting like us. They are actors pretending to be something they are not. And once they have gained our trust, they spew their deceit.

Just to give a Biblical example of how easy they enter, take Judas Iscariot. He was chosen among the twelve by Jesus Christ Himself. Christ knew who Judas was and that Judas had a mission to betray Him. The Bible states, *"Jesus answered them, Have not I chosen you twelve, and one of you is a devil? He spake of Judas Iscariot the son of Simon: for he it was that should betray him, being one of the twelve."* John 6:70-71. So it is obvious that Christ knew there was an unbeliever in the group. But did the disciples know?

The answer to that question can be found in Matthew 26. Christ mentioned while eating with the disciples during the Passover that one of them would betray Him. Immediately they all became sad and began to question one by one to the Lord, *"Is it I?"* By their statement, they must not have known. But how could they miss who it was?

Judas was good at acting the part. His actions seemed to concern the group's betterment; he walked and talked with them and never spoke against Christ, as far as we know. It seems he did everything he was told to do. The obedience

36

and concern he portrayed could have been why they didn't know. Let me give you some examples.

First, I'm sure that the disciples had no idea that Judas was a betrayer because Christ Himself gave Judas the right to carry the money bag. After all, who, knowing that someone is a thief and a betrayer, would do that? The disciples had often seen where Christ knew the hearts and minds of the people. That being so, surely He wouldn't let a thief and traitor hold all the money. They didn't know that Judas had a significant role to play, and it wasn't what the disciples expected. He was to betray the Son of God.

In John chapter 12, we find Judas sounding like he was a good steward of the money entrusted to him. The setting was when Mary came with a bottle of ointment to pour on Christ. The oil was costly, and even the container she used and broke was expensive. Mary did this out of love and appreciation for what the Lord had done for her. Maybe not knowing the full meaning of it, she also did it according to Christ for His burial.

When Judas saw Mary break the container and pour it on the Lord's feet, he said, *"Why was not this ointment sold for three hundred pence, and given to the poor?"* John 12:5. Sounds spiritual and caring for others, doesn't it? I'm sure his actions in the disciples' eyes seemed pure and right.

However, Christ knowing the heart and mind, knew Judas' true intentions. The Bible shows this in verse six, *"This he said, not that he cared for the poor; but because he was a thief, and had the bag, and bare what was put therein."*

Judas had no concern whatsoever for the poor. He was greedy and wanted to keep the money. See how easy it is for someone to fool others into believing they have a pure heart and good intentions for the church? This gives a lot of meaning to the statement, "The road to Hell is paved with good intentions." It's not the intentions that are important; the motive to please the Lord and do His will is what's important. If the men with Christ physically didn't recognize an unbeliever coming against the faith, how much more should we be diligent?

We have allowed people like Judas in many of our churches today because of the world's push for love and tolerance. We don't want the stigma that can come with standing true to the truth of God's Word. For the most part, we have failed to teach the believer about being sanctified.

Jude, talking of these people that crept in and are corrupting the church, says, "...who were before of old ordained to this condemnation..."

Some people read into this passage that God has pre-ordained that certain evil-doers be condemned. That simply cannot be the case because God doesn't want anyone to perish. I believe the passage is referring to the fact that these people do what they do, fully knowing the punishment because God had already warned them what would happen to people who commit such acts. I believe we can see this in the next few verses.

God is a loving just God who always has pre-warned judgment by giving us rules and what will happen if they are broken. He did this in the Garden of Eden with man concerning the Fruit of Knowledge. He did it with the children of Israel when He gave Moses the Law and all the ordinances He wanted to be obeyed. He even did it to Pharaoh before sending the plagues to Egypt.

Man brings condemnation to himself because he willfully and knowingly disobeys God's Word. God has no choice but to condemn because He is a God that cannot lie. When He says if you do such and such, you will face such and such, He must honor His Word. You can't do wrong and get by.

It was also forewritten for the people in the future. God has warned in Revelation and other places what will take place and what will happen to people who refuse to repent and obey Him.

I always hear the statement, "If God is such a loving and good God, why does He send people to hell?" The answer is quite simple; HE DOESN'T. Man chooses his own destiny. God loved us so much that He sent His very Son to prevent us from facing the wrath and punishment of God. It's up to man to follow the path God has laid out. And no, the devil didn't make you do it; you did it out of your own free will. As my parents always said, "You made your bed, and you will have to lay in it."

Let me just give a few scriptures to back my claim.

God warned in Romans 6:23. *"For the wages of sin is death; but the gift of God is eternal life through Jesus Christ our Lord."*

In 1ˢᵗ Corinthians 10:13, God tells us that there is a way out. *"There hath no temptation taken you but such as is common to man: but God is faithful, who will not suffer you to be tempted above that ye are able; but will with the temptation also make a way to escape, that ye may be able to bear it."*

Galatians 5:19-21 tells us the works of sin and its consequence. *"Now the works of the flesh are manifest, which are these; Adultery, fornication, uncleanness, lasciviousness, Idolatry, witchcraft, hatred, variance, emulations, wrath, strife, seditions, heresies, Envyings, murders, drunkenness, revellings, and such like: of the which I tell you before, as I have also told you in time past, that they which do such things shall not inherit the kingdom of God."*

1ˢᵗ John 1:9 shows us how to be free from sin. *"If we confess our sins, he is faithful and just to forgive us our sins, and to cleanse us from all unrighteousness."*

Colossians 3:5-6 let's us know we must do our part. *"Mortify therefore your members which are upon the earth; fornication, uncleanness, inordinate affection, evil concupiscence, and covetousness, which is idolatry: For which things' sake the wrath of God cometh on the children of disobedience..."*

I believe these scriptures alone can be proof enough that God has warned us of any condemnation that man will face and what he can do about it.

Jude called these people *"ungodly men."* Proverbs 16:27 tells the attitude of ungodly men, *"An ungodly man diggeth up evil: and in his lips there is as a burning fire."* The ungodly men in the original language mean irreverent or wicked. These people were without true religion or any piety, although they tried to show themselves as having it.

These people had no desire to worship God truly. Timothy was warning us about these people in 2nd Timothy 3:5, *"Having a form of godliness, but denying the power thereof: from such turn away."*

These "ungodly men" were *"turning the grace of our God into lasciviousness."* Paul said in Ephesians 2:8, *"For by grace are ye saved through faith; and that not of yourselves: it is the gift of God…"* We can never meet God's satisfaction without grace. They were taking the very thing that brings us unto salvation and polluting its meaning.

Lasciviousness typically means overt and offensive sexual desire, but it also can reach into other sinful indulgences. In essence, they were saying that now you have been saved by the grace of God, you can do and live as you want, and it will be okay.

As a Baptist, I hear many people misunderstand our Baptist beliefs because we, as Baptists, believe that once a person is saved, he is saved eternally, and nothing will change that, thus, the term "once saved, always saved." But that is not the meaning of eternal salvation at all. It is never meant to say we are free to sin because we have been saved by grace.

Although it is true that once an individual accepts the grace of God, they are forever in the family of God, it is still essential that we try our best to live a life pleasing to God and keep ourselves pure. No, we are not saved by works, but our lifestyle should represent that we are saved in how we live it.

The belief that once we are saved by grace, we no longer have to obey the Mosaic Law or keep the ten commandments really began to flourish in the 3rd century through Gnosticism. But as stated before, the concept was already in existence in Jude's day.

From the very beginning, man has tried to circumvent having to obey God. We, by nature, don't like being told what to do. We, by nature, are greedy and want everything we see. A two-year-old is a prime example of this. You don't have to teach him greed and selfishness; it is born in him, and he will show that when it comes to sharing his toys with other children.

Man has always twisted the Word of God to his advantage as well. We, as humans, try to take away or add to key scriptures to form what we want them to say. Satan, who started all of that, used it on Eve and Christ Himself. He used Scripture and turned it around to make it appear to be approval of things against God.

So it only seems natural that man would use something as pure as grace and try to twist its original intent. But Paul makes it plain that just because we are saved doesn't give us a license to sin. Romans 6:1-2 states, *"What shall we say then? Shall we continue in sin, that grace may abound? God forbid. How shall we, that are dead to sin, live any longer therein?"*

All through the book of Romans, you will find Paul coming against the idea that we can do as we please now that we have the grace of God in our lives. Just as oil and water don't mix, neither do holiness and unholiness. We are freed **from** our sin, not free **to** sin.

It's bad enough to profane the wonderful grace of God, but they further their actions by *"denying the only Lord God, and our Lord Jesus Christ."* The denying here is in the passive, which means something has caused them to deny God. What caused it was the desire to serve their senses more than worship God.

This can be interpreted as only denying Jesus Christ, or it can be, as I see it, denying God and Jesus Christ. Either way, if you deny one, you have denied all of the Godhead, God the Father, God the Son, and God the Holy Ghost, for all three are in one.

It is incredible that this kind of behavior took place just a little over 30 years since Christ died and rose again. It is said that by the 2nd century, the pagans twisted Christian vocabulary to involve atheism (no idols), cannibalism (eating the Lord's body and drinking his blood), immorality (growing out of a sensual conception of the word love), and magic and sorcery (in baptism and the Lord's Supper). How could they have strayed so far away in just those short years of walking and talking with Jesus Christ, God in the flesh?

The same question could have been asked to Adam and Eve. Or what about the people that walked with Christ, saw His miracles, ate the divine food He supplied in the wilderness, and yet turned against Him and crucified Him? It can also be asked of us individually. How long after you were born again and were filled with the Holy Spirit of God did it take for you to commit a sin?

This flesh we live in is so drawn to its desires that it takes continual prayer and self-denial to live even close to what God would have us live. Paul put it this way in Romans 7:21-24, *"I find then a law, that, when I would do good, evil is present with me. For I delight in the law of God after the inward man: But I see another law in my members, warring against the law of my mind, and bringing me into captivity to the law of sin which is in my members. O wretched man that I am! who shall deliver me from the body of this death?"* Sound like something you might struggle with daily? I would say so!

Some of our modern preachers on television today have denied God and Christ by what they preach. When on interviews with people like Oprah Winfrey, they have said that there are many ways to God. That, my friend, is denying Jesus Christ, because Christ said, *"...I am **the** way, **the** truth, and **the** life: **no man cometh** unto the Father, **but by me.**"* John 14:6.

1st Timothy 2:5 makes it even plainer to understand; *"For there is **one God**, and **one mediator** between God and men, **the man Christ Jesus;**..."*

John 10:1-9 explains that anyone that comes any other way is the same as a thief and a robber, and Christ is the only door we can enter to get to the Father, *"Verily, verily, I say unto you, He that entereth not by the door into the sheepfold, but climbeth up some other way, the same is a thief and a robber. But he that entereth in by the door is the shepherd of the sheep. To him the porter openeth; and the sheep hear his voice: and he calleth his own sheep by name, and leadeth them out. And when he putteth forth his own sheep, he goeth before them, and the sheep follow him: for they know his voice. And a stranger will they not follow, but will flee from him: for they know not the voice of strangers. This parable spake Jesus unto them: but they understood not what things they were which he spake unto them. Then said Jesus unto them again, Verily, verily, I say unto you, I am the door of the sheep. "* Only those that have put their trust in Christ Jesus and Him alone will be able to hear his voice and enter Heaven.

I truly believe that these false teachers had never had a personal relationship with Jesus Christ. I believe they had never surrendered their life to Him and had the Holy Spirit live and guide inside of them.

It would be wise for you to examine yourself closely and view your life to see if it aligns with Christ. Examine if your heart wants to be holy and pleasing to God.

Salvation doesn't come by a simple, repeated prayer. But by having a broken heart about your sinful condition and a desire to turn away from that lifestyle. Then understand what immeasurable love Christ had to die for your rotten sinful condition and trust in His power to save you through His blood that He shed on the cross and the resurrection of His body again so you can die to yourself and live unto Him.

Have you made that commitment? Today would be a good day to do so.

Chapter 5

Three Strikes and You're Out

"I will therefore put you in remembrance, though ye once knew this, how that the Lord, having saved the people out of the land of Egypt, afterward destroyed them that believed not. And the angels which kept not their first estate, but left their own habitation, he hath reserved in everlasting chains under darkness unto the judgment of the great day. Even as Sodom and Gomorrha, and the cities about them in like manner, giving themselves over to fornication, and going after strange flesh, are set forth for an example, suffering the vengeance of eternal fire." Jude verses 5-7.

In these three verses, Jude wants to remind the people what God did to those who didn't follow what God said. *"I will therefore put you in remembrance, though ye once knew this...."* The examples Jude gave were something that every Jewish person should have already known in the first place.

The Jews are very traditional people. They have been told down throughout their generations stories of Abraham, Moses, and other patriarchs, along with what the people of old went through. These stories should have been, and most likely were, in their minds already. But Jude wanted to refresh those memories and to make them come alive again in their minds.

It reminds me of a person that has a heart attack because of bad eating habits. When the event actually took place, the

47

pain and suffering were fresh in their mind. For a little while, you would not be able to get them to eat unhealthy food if you tried. But as time passes, life happens, and the pain and suffering have taken a big back seat in their minds. When that happens, they often begin to eat unhealthily again. It's not because they don't know what would and did happen; it has just been replaced with today's problems and therefore doesn't bare as much weight as it did when they had the heart attack.

It has happened to most of us Christians as well. When God gloriously saved our souls, the days immediately after were such a change from the life we lived before. We wanted to live right and tell everybody what God had done for us. Our burden of sin had been lifted, and joy filled our hearts.

But once we get back to work and bills become due, life puts stress on us, and people begin to mock our experience; before we know it, we have lost that joy and drive to be a good witness for our Lord and Savior. We can recall and know for sure in our minds that God saved us, but the freshness of that experience has taken a back seat to the present day's problems.

Another way you understand what Jude is trying to say is when families have reunions or birthdays. As a family, all the people present had experienced stories and events that had taken place in the past. But when those stories began to be re-told, it is almost like you were transported back to the day the event took place. This is where Jude wanted to get his people to go. Remembering in detail as if it was the day it happened.

The areas Jude wanted them to remember weren't pleasant thoughts. It was times in their history when God had to send judgment, not only to them but even to God's angels. He is about to remind them that there is more to God than just His love and mercy. He gives three examples for them to think about. Each starts out well but ends in devastation.

It is kind of like baseball. When the final batter gets up in the last inning of the game, he can either hit the ball out of the park or keep missing the mark and be called out. If he strikes out, his time is over, and he can't take the time back again to make a difference, and he has ended the game for everyone on his team in defeat. May we all strive to hit the ball out of the park, so to speak, for Christ.

The first remembrance that Jude mentioned is something every Jewish person knew well, " ...*how that the Lord, having saved the people out of the land of Egypt, afterward destroyed them that believed not.*"

In Exodus 12:40-42, we read about when the children of Israel dwelt in Egypt. *"Now the sojourning of the children of Israel, who dwelt in Egypt, was four hundred and thirty years. And it came to pass at the end of the four hundred and thirty years, even the selfsame day it came to pass, that all the hosts of the LORD went out from the land of Egypt. It is a night to be much observed unto the LORD for bringing them out from the land of Egypt: this is that night of the LORD to be observed of all the children of Israel in their generations."*

I believe that Jude started with this because it deals with Abraham, the father of the Jews. If there was anything they should know about, it was their heritage. Moses described 656 years of world history in just six chapters, from creation to the flood. However, he took nineteen chapters that covered only 175 years to give the history of Abraham. Can you now understand how vital their heritage's history is to them? Unquestionably every Jew during the time of Jude's writing knew of these events in detail.

To summarize, up unto this point, God had promised Abraham that He would bless him and raise a nation by his seed, in which all the earth would be blessed.

Abraham, at first, had difficulty believing this because his wife was barren, and both of them were well advanced in years. Still, eventually, Abraham took God at His word and trusted everything God had promised.

Abraham further showed his faith in God when God told him to offer his very son Isaac, through whom all these promises were to be fulfilled on an altar for a sacrifice. When you read the story of this event, you can see Abraham's faith that God would fulfill His promise even if it meant God would raise Isaac from the dead.

"And it came to pass after these things, that God did tempt Abraham, and said unto him, Abraham: and he said, Behold, here I am. And he said, Take now thy son, thine only son Isaac, whom thou lovest, and get thee into the land of Moriah; and offer him there for a burnt offering upon one of the mountains which I will tell thee of. And Abraham rose up early in the morning, and saddled his ass, and took two of

*his young men with him, and Isaac his son, and clave the wood for the burnt offering, and rose up, and went unto the place of which God had told him. Then on the third day Abraham lifted up his eyes, and saw the place afar off. And Abraham said unto his young men, Abide ye here with the ass; and I and the lad will go yonder and worship, **and come again to you.*** " Genesis 22:1-5.

Notice the last phrase, *"and come again to you."* I truly believe Abraham was referring to him and Isaac returning. Notice also that it was Abraham's only son, so if God didn't work a miracle, the promise would have ended there. This story alone should give us confidence that God will accomplish what He wants, even if He has us walk through areas that seem impossible.

As time went by, famine in the land brought Abraham to travel to Egypt. Egypt controlled Canaan at that time. Later, we see where some of Abraham's descendants even sold Joseph into slavery. But God still had a plan.

I won't take the time to go over all the events. Still, the bottom line, Joseph, even though sold into slavery, even though he had also been thrown into prison, and even though the promise seemed impossible, was used to keep the seed of Abraham alive so the promise could be fulfilled. If you haven't read the events, or it has been a while since you have, I suggest you read the entire story. The events are told in Genesis, chapters 39-50. When you read it over, you will find God over and over confirming the promise even in the midst of troubles.

As you read further in the Scriptures, you will see the problems didn't stop but got worse. Yes, God brought this handful of people to Egypt. Yes, God was going to make a great nation out of them. However, in the time between them being brought into position to get the promise until it is delivered, there would be many obstacles, even them becoming slaves in the very land God sent them to.

Many interpret the verses in Exodus 12 as the Israelites being in bondage as slaves in Egypt during the entire time. But this is referring to when Abraham received the promise from God in Geneses 12:1-20 until they were delivered out of Egypt. In Geneses 15:13, we see that it is a total of four hundred years that they would be afflicted. *"And he said unto Abram, Know of a surety that thy seed shall be a stranger in a land that is not theirs, and shall serve them; and they shall afflict them four hundred years..."* Notice, that was the affliction period, not slavery. But slavery would eventually become a reality. Many historians believe the actual time of slavery was around 130 years.

So why would God allow His chosen people, that He made a promise to bless and multiply, to move into such hardship? In those 400 years, the family of Israel grew from a tiny band of 70 people into a nation. By being in bondage, the Israelites were held in one place so they could eventually become a nation. He would use the same people that put them into slavery to bless them with great wealth. God would also use all the events to show the world that He was not only on His chosen people's side but that He would take care of them. And for me, most importantly, it should have given them faith in God that God will deliver and make good all He says no matter who comes against it.

There was also a time frame God had to take care of first. Genesis 15:14-16, *"And also that nation, whom they shall serve, will I judge: and afterward shall they come out with great substance. And thou shalt go to thy fathers in peace; thou shalt be buried in a good old age. But in the fourth generation they shall come hither again: for the iniquity of the Amorites is not yet full."*

One of the reasons that God's people were put into slavery was because they were growing in such great numbers that Pharoh became nervous they would take over. God was doing what He promised, making them into a great nation. Even though Pharoh tried to make them work harder and put restrictions on them to discourage their population growth, they grew more prominent. A lesson to learn here is that not everyone will be happy about God blessing you. There are people who are jealous of God's favor in our lives.

Not everything we go through is because of sin; sometimes God is trying to show His power. Have you ever walked through dark times in your life and wondered why God would allow you to go through them? Maybe you complained to Him, saying you had done nothing to have to go through such a trial. Well, just maybe, God is trying to make you stronger or show the world His tremendous power of love, protection, and deliverance. Perhaps He is using the events in your life to deal with others. One thing for sure, *"all things work together for good to them that love God, to them who are the called according to his purpose."* Romans 8:28. God has a reason for every season.

God finally allowed His chosen to escape Egypt's bondage. It has been argued that the number of the remnant that escaped Egypt was anywhere between 30,000 to two and a half million. Yes, the Bible mentions an army of 600,000 strong men, not including women and children. But, historians and scholars have argued the interpretation of the original Hebrew, of which none has proven to be correct.

Both have a strong case; some believe the literal interpretation to mean thousands, and others do not. God was not concerned with the numbers and, in some places, told them not to number themselves. God was focused on showing His power and the promises He made to the children of Israel. If God doesn't think it important about the number, neither should we.

You would think that after all the children of Israel went through and God miraculously delivered them out of the hands of the Egyptians, they would follow God's Word and commandments. It should also be noted that they could have saved themselves 40 more years of hardship if they had just obeyed what God had told them to do.

The people that came out of Egypt saw God's provision, protection, and deliverance. They knew of God's promises, yet they turned against God and refused to believe. That is what still happens today. Mankind sees the hand of God. They can see His protection. Many hear of God's promise that if we just put our trust in His Son's death, burial and resurrection, we could escape the judgment, but many still refuse and turn away from God and won't believe.

Only two of the original people who were delivered out of Egypt lived to go into the promised land, Joshua and Caleb. They were able to go in because of their faith in God. The only way any of us will make it through is by having faith in God.

There is another central point I cannot in good conscience leave out that Jude reminded the people of. Jude made this statement, *"...having saved the people out of the land of Egypt, afterward destroyed them that believed not..."* Now before I go on, I want to be perfectly clear that I belong to a Baptist church. We believe that we are saved through the blood of Christ, not of works. We do not believe that anyone can work their way to Heaven. However, I must bring some of these things up so you can understand the gravity of Jude's warning.

Egypt is a type of this world and the bondage it has over mankind. Jude reminded the people that God had brought them out of that bondage. So how did He do that? God told the people that if they wanted to escape the bondage of Egypt and the wrath of God, they must sacrifice a lamb, take the blood, and put it on the doorpost of their home. Anyone that didn't believe and apply the blood would perish. *They must believe in the blood and apply it to their dwelling.* Once they applied the blood, they were safe from the wrath of God. The death angel passed, and all those that had the blood applied survived.

Next, after having the blood applied and they came out of Egypt (this world's bondage), they went through a type of baptism by walking through the Red Sea. It was divided, and water was all about them. Then after coming through the Red Sea, God gave Moses His rules and commandments that they should follow. From then on, their faith was tested by this world through obstacles they faced.

To me, that was the perfect picture of how we are saved today. We must first be warned that the wrath of God has been sentenced toward us. If we want to escape that wrath, we must believe in the sacrificial blood of Christ and apply it to our hearts (dwelling). Then we are instructed to follow in believer's baptism as a sign that we are dead to this world and alive in Christ. We then begin to learn what God expects from us, and Satan daily begins to test our faith.

Like today's believers, they were saved by the blood and not of anything they could have done without the blood. So if they were saved out of the bondage of this world, why they didn't make it to their spiritual heaven? Their type of heaven was the promised land, the land flowing with milk and honey, the land in and around Canaan. We sing songs today of Heaven as our Canaan land.

They made it to where they were near their promised land, the lamb's blood had delivered them, but something happened to cause, as stated before, only two of the original people to make it out of Egypt and inside the promised land.

Here is where the trouble began. God told Moses to choose twelve "leaders" out of the twelve tribes of Israel to go and spy on the land that God had promised. Notice these were leaders, not just ordinary people. These were leaders that the people listened to and who gave instructions to the people; they were the "heads" of Israel.

After the "leaders" spied on the land, they came back and told the people that the land indeed flowed with milk and honey, and they even had a cluster of grapes to show proof of it. But "ten" of these leaders of the people, instead of being like Caleb, one of the leaders, added falsehood to the story saying the land had *"...eateth up the inhabitants thereof; and all the people that we saw in it are men of a great stature....we were in our own sight as grasshoppers, and so we were in their sight."* Numbers 13:32-33.

This, in turn, brought fear to the people. Instead of trusting in God's promise, they leaned on their own power and felt it better to return to their old ways in Egypt (the world). They had lost faith in all that God had done for them. They even got together to try and overthrow Moses and elect a captain that would take them back to Egypt.

Joshua and Caleb told the people that they could possess the land but must not turn against God. *"And Joshua the son of Nun, and Caleb the son of Jephunneh, which were of them that searched the land, rent their clothes: And they spake unto all the company of the children of Israel, saying, The land, which we passed through to search it, is an exceeding good land. If the LORD delight in us, then he will bring us into this land, and give it us; a land which floweth with milk and honey. Only rebel not ye against the LORD, neither fear ye the people of the land; for they are bread for us: their defence is departed from them, and the LORD is with us: fear them not."* Numbers 14:6-9.

Instead of believing Joshua, Caleb, and God, they chose to believe the leaders that gave a false report. Remember, these ten were leaders of the congregation. They twisted what they saw and turned against God's Words and promises. Because of that, many of the people of God believed the false reports. They turned against God and were even going to stone Joshua and Caleb, who spoke the truth of God.

Then God told the people who rejected His Word that all those who had turned against Him would die in the wilderness. The only ones that God said would make it to their promised land would be Joshua and Caleb out of all those numbered coming out of Egypt. It would do you good to read the events in Numbers chapters 13 & 14 to get all of the details.

Remember again, the people God destroyed in the wilderness had been brought out of Egypt by the blood of a lamb, followed by a type of baptism, and received God's instructions. No matter if you believe in eternal salvation or not, I think I would heed the warning that Jude gave and make sure you are doing your best to live as the Lord would have you live. God has given us the power of the Holy Spirit to do so. No, we won't be perfect, but our hearts, where God judges, should be bent toward pleasing Him instead of going back to the world we came from.

These examples of God's ancient judgments need to be our warnings and examples as well. His holiness is the same as ever, His justice and hatred of sin are the same, and His power to avenge it is the same as ever. His judgments now may be more spiritual, but they are not less terrible.

Jude then moves on to the celestial realm. *"And the angels which kept not their first estate, but left their own habitation, he hath reserved in everlasting chains under darkness unto the judgment of the great day." Jude verse 6.*

Here again, there is a large debate on who these angels were and where they were at the time of leaving. Some believe this is talking about when Satan was cast out and drew a third of Heaven's host with him. Others believe these are the "sons of God" mentioned in Genesis 6:2. In the latter belief, these angels, according to some, saw the women on earth and lusted after them; therefore, they willingly gave up the position God had given them so they could satisfy their lust for these women.

This debate has been going on for centuries. I am about to venture, as Star Trek would say, "Where no man has ever gone before." Now, before I do this, I want to make one thing clear. I just want you to understand where the ideology of the latter is coming from and why people believe what they do about this. I am in no wise saying that I agree with the opinions, nor should you base yours on what I write. You need to pray to God for the Holy Spirit to give you wisdom and understanding. NEVER base your opinion of the Bible on what a man says, no matter how much they seem to know or are respected. ALWAYS study and pray for God's guidance. Man is fallible, but God isn't. That being said, let's see if we can gather where this opinion came from.

As you will see later in this book, Jude makes a direct quote from the book of Enoch in verse 14. As a matter of fact, the end of verse six in Jude is spoken about in the book of Enoch, chapter 10 (one of the Apocryphal books). The mentioning of the punishment of these angels in Enoch chapter 10 is a result of what was written in the book of Enoch Chapter 7 [sect. II.2].

In order not to make this a long in-depth coverage of the whole story, I will give you a brief summary. According to the book of Enoch, there were angels that God had given authority to throughout the universe, it appears. But, when these angels saw how beautiful the women on earth were, they decided to give up their heavenly positions so they could come to earth, take these women and have sexual relationships with them.

According to the book of Enoch, the one that had first made the decision to do this ungodly act was the leader named Samyaza. But he didn't want to take the judgment that might come alone, so he convinced the others to make an oath to do the same. The total that rebelled, according to the book of Enoch, was two hundred.

From this decision and actions of these angels, according to the book of Enoch, is how giants came about. It also describes these angels teaching men how to fight and make weapons and teaching mankind how to do sorcery, astrology, and idol worship.

According to Jewish mythology, these giants, half-human, and half-divine, are known as the Nephilim.

According to the book of Enoch, these supposedly were the offspring of the giants that came from the relations with earthly women, and these were where evil spirits came from.

The debate is because of what is written in the book of Enoch and how some people interpret Genesis 6:1-4, *"And it came to pass, when men began to multiply on the face of the earth, and daughters were born unto them, That the sons of God saw the daughters of men that they were fair; and they took them wives of all which they chose. And the LORD said, My spirit shall not always strive with man, for that he also is flesh: yet his days shall be an hundred and twenty years. There were giants in the earth in those days; and also after that, when the sons of God came in unto the daughters of men, and they bare children to them, the same became mighty men which were of old, men of renown."*

Many believe that the "sons of God" were these rebellious angels. There are, however, two other main beliefs about who the "sons of God" are. One is they are men whom God had made powerful human rulers. The other central belief is that they were godly descendants of Seth intermarrying with the wicked descendants of Cain.

From all the information I have now given, I am sure that understanding who the "sons of God" are is as clear as mud. Right? Before you decide on your beliefs, please wait until we cover a direct quote from Jude from Enoch's book later in this study. There, we will give you more information about the book of Enoch and other material that will shed more light on whether to believe all that is written or not in its pages.

Once again, the Bible doesn't explain who these angels are entirely, but we can gather from the verse that they somehow had a position with God with which they weren't satisfied. They willfully turned against God, so they must have had free will. Most don't believe these angels are a part of the third of angles that were cast out of heaven. The reason being, these angels chose to give up their position, and the fallen angels of Satan were thrown out of heaven. What we know is that because they didn't keep their faith and obedience to God, they will face the judgment of God.

It is because of the way Jude begins verse 7 that many interpret that the angels had lusted after the women of earth and sinned by fornicating with them. *"Even as Sodom and Gomorrha, and the cities about them in like manner, giving themselves over to fornication, and going after strange flesh,* are set forth for an example, suffering the vengeance of eternal fire."* Jude verse 7.

You can see how they could interpret the Scripture that way. *"Even as Sodom and Gomorrha"* seem to be a parallel example of what some believe the angels had done; *"going after strange flesh."* But you can also take it as them leaving their standing and deliberately sinning against God. Therefore, they, too, will face the judgment of God. I think God proves this in Luke 17:32, *"Remember Lot's wife."* She was an example to every one of sin's consequences of turning away from God and fulfilling the desires of the flesh or the love of it.

Once again, it must not be God's primary focus in letting us know which is right; His focus is that if you turn against Him, you **will** face judgment. We do know, however, that

62

demons don't want to go to the abyss; you can tell that when reading the story of Jesus talking to the demons which possessed the two men of Gergesenes found in Matthew chapter 8. And by the way, the darkness here means an absence of light. The absence of light is the absence of God. I wouldn't imagine anyone or anything would want to be in a place where God is not there to intervene and control.

Jude further drives this point home in verse 7, talking about Sodom and Gomorrha and the cities around them. The story of Sodom and Gomorrha started in Genesis chapter 13. Abraham and Lot had become so blessed by God that trouble began to arise between their herdsmen, so Abraham decided it best they find land for themselves.

Abraham gave Lot the choice of what to pick. In Genesis 13:10, you can see why Lot chose the place he did, *"And Lot lifted up his eyes, and beheld all the plain of Jordan, that it was well watered every where, before the LORD destroyed Sodom and Gomorrah, even as the garden of the LORD, like the land of Egypt, as thou comest unto Zoar."*

Lot chose with his eyes and his earthly rationality. The verse described the area as *"well watered every where...even as the garden of the LORD."* In man's eyes, that would be a perfect place to make a living for his family since he was a shepherd. Not only did it have a great water supply, but the land was well nourished, so much so that it resembled the Garden of Eden.

But just because the grass is greener on the other side doesn't mean it's where you should go. Instead of seeking God's advice, Lot used his experience and knowledge.

63

Instead of listening to God with his heart, he picked an area with the desire of his eyes.

The problem that Lot didn't count the cost on is found in Genesis chapter 13:13, *"But the men of Sodom were wicked and sinners before the LORD exceedingly."* These men weren't just sinners but sinned exceedingly.

To give you a better idea of how bad they were, I want to give a quote from Adam Clarks Commentary. "A sinner is one who is ever aiming at happiness and constantly missing his mark; because, being wicked-radically evil within, every affection and passion depraved and out of order, he seeks for happiness where it never can be found, in worldly honors and possessions, and in sensual gratifications, the end of which is disappointment, affliction, vexation, and ruin...This, however, amounts to no more than the common character of sinful man; but the people of Sodom were exceedingly sinful and wicked before, or against, the Lord-they were sinners of no common character; **they excelled in unrighteousness** and soon filled up the measure of their iniquities."

To show how deranged these people became, even when God's angels struck them with blindness, they continued to try and do evil. Have you ever been disciplined by God yet continued to do your evil deed? Today's society has made it easy to do. Countless people are addicted to sinful things: pornography, alcohol, adultery, and the like.

With modern society, it has become easy and can be done in secrecy. But don't be fooled, God is a watchful eye, and nothing is hidden from His sight. God tries to warn us before sending judgment. Just as God warned Lot to get out of his sinful condition in Genesis chapter 19:12, *"And the men said unto Lot, Hast thou here any besides? son in law, and thy sons, and thy daughters, and whatsoever thou hast in the city, bring them out of this place..."* God has warned all of us to do the same in Revelation 18:4, *"And I heard another voice from heaven, saying, Come out of her, my people, that ye be not partakers of her sins, and that ye receive not of her plagues."*

2nd Peter 2:7 gives us the reason that Lot was spared from this judgment, *"And delivered just Lot, vexed with the filthy conversation of the wicked..."* The conditions that Lot was living in were disgusting to him and made him sick to his stomach. We should view sin the same way. The only question I have is, how many people did Lot witness to warning them of the coming destruction? I ask myself that same question about myself. How many people have I warned about the wrath and judgment of God to all that disobey Him?

Many people will say that Sodom and Gomorrah were destroyed because of homosexuality. But that is not what the Scripture is teaching. Although homosexuality may result from living a totally sinful life, the main reason that brought on the judgment was their continual evil, destructive behavior without any thought or repentance. They were wealthy and lived in a land full of blessings, but they became self-centered, and their eyes were on pleasure instead of giving God glory for what He had given and, because of that, living and trusting in Him.

It was no different than the Garden of Eden. Adam and Eve were in the perfect place. They were blessed beyond measure. But they weren't content and wanted more. Because of greed and disobedience to God, they received judgment.

Lot may not have known what kind of wickedness and troubles lay ahead of him because of his decision. That is why it is paramount that we pray for God's direction before embarking on big decisions in our lives. He knows the beginning to the ending and all in between. He knows what is best for us. If we want to stay away from judgment, we need to trust in Him and be willing servants.

We don't know why Lot didn't pack and move once he found how wicked the people were, but later on, the Bible reveals that Lot had become a central figure in the town. The end result of his decision cost him his wife and all of his belongings. YOU PLAY WITH FIRE, AND YOU WILL GET BURNT!

2nd Peter 2 also gives three examples. But instead of using Egypt, he used the example of the flood; *"And spared not the old world, but saved Noah the eighth person, a preacher of righteousness, bringing in the flood upon the world of the ungodly..."* The eighth person simply meant the last of the eight to go into the ark.

Many people have used Jude's examples to show that we can lose our salvation, but I don't see it that way. I view it that we all, in the beginning, have the freedom to choose God's ways or reject them. Everyone that believed in God made it, and those that didn't face judgment. It was their **faith in God** that made the difference. Hebrews 11:7 backs that up, *"By faith Noah, being warned of God of things not seen as yet, moved with fear, prepared an ark to the saving of his house; by the which he condemned the world, and became heir of the righteousness which is by faith."*

I still believe Romans 10:13, *"For whosoever shall call upon the name of the Lord shall be saved."* That being said, it would behoove us to make sure we have truly accepted Him and examine our lives to ensure we are doing our best at being holy and righteous before Him.

Chapter 6

No Respect

"Likewise also these filthy dreamers defile the flesh, despise dominion, and speak evil of dignities. Yet Michael the archangel, when contending with the devil he disputed about the body of Moses, durst not bring against him a railing accusation, but said, The Lord rebuke thee."
Jude verses 8-9.

Jude begins verse 8 with another comparable word, *"likewise."* This term means a similarity. He wants the people to understand that what he is about to say next can be compared to the description and the results of things he just discussed. He had just talked about the children of Israel, the angels, and the sodomites' evil doings and rebellion against God and how they were punished because of their not trusting and following God.

The things he had mentioned happened many years before what was taking place in the church during Jude's writing. He wanted his people to know the same thing would apply to those of his day if they walked in the paths of the people referenced.

Hebrews 13:8 states, *"Jesus Christ the same yesterday, and to day, and for ever."* God's ways are set in stone. God's laws and standards do not change no matter how much society changes. Just because society says something is okay doesn't change how God feels about it.

I remember when I was younger. My parents raised us in a Christian home. We went to church every time the door was opened. As children, we were not allowed to listen to secular music, have poker cards in the home, curse, go to movies, go swimming with the opposite sex, and the list goes on.

We also lived in what was called "a blue state." Many states back in those days adopted laws that respected God's Word. Restaurants and most gas stations would close on Sundays. You could not buy alcoholic beverages on Sunday, nor did they allow grocery stores to sell alcohol.

But as the years went by, things began to change. Grocery stores started selling alcoholic beverages, restaurants and gas stations began to open, movies were packed on Sundays, and even the television stations became bolder in airing things with adult content. It seemed everywhere you looked, the floodgates of secularism had flooded our society.

Many Christians tried to stand against this by refusing to buy groceries at any store selling alcoholic beverages. A lot of Christians also would boycott certain movies and shows on television and Disney by not watching them or buying their products; some even removed their televisions from their home.

But as time went on, you couldn't find a grocery store that didn't sell alcoholic beverages, forcing Christians to buy there anyway if they wanted to have food in the home. Risque television commercials and movies dulled the senses of people's moral values to the point they would watch things that in the past would appall them. And with the cost of everything rising, both parents had to work, causing less time, so it began convenient to eat out on Sunday rather than have a meal prepared the day before and eat it on Sunday.

Now, in 2022, you would think we are living in Sodom and Gomorrah. Anything goes anymore. But although our society accepts it as the norm, God is still against it and expects His statutes to be honored, or you will face His judgment. He would not be considered politically correct by today's standards.

Jude faced the same problem that we Americans faced, and just as in America, these attitudes and actions were in the church itself.

Now he begins to show how these people are compared to the others who had lived in the past. The text called them *"filthy dreamers."* It should be noted that the word "filthy" is not in the original, and it was added in the KJV so we could better understand.

Dreams, in the normal sense of the word, are not evil. It took dreamers to find a way to invent a car, a plane, the telephone, cell phones, and every other modern convenience that we have today. Dreamers set out to find a new world where Christians could worship God in freedom, which eventually led to the forming of a new nation, America. It took dreamers to get us to the moon and space exploration like never known before.

Humanity's values have been strengthened because of dreamers. A perfect example of this is Dr. Marin Luther King Jr. During his days, black people suffered greatly.

They were not allowed to drink water from public fountains and couldn't go to public restrooms that were not allocated for them. They couldn't vote or hold good jobs. They weren't allowed to enter restaurants at the front door, sit at the tables, or take the front seat of city buses. They were often beaten, hung, and harassed without anyone taking their defense.

But one day, a dreamer named Martin Luther King Jr. decided to make a difference. He could see a better society for everyone in his mind, and he could see this happening without having his people take up arms and fight. His dream was for "ALL" people, not just his own. He delivered this idea to the American people in a speech called "I Have a Dream," and what better place to deliver it than at the Lincoln Memorial in Washington, D.C.

He dreamed that the nation he lived in would eventually understand the meaning of what it was founded upon: that "all men are created equal." Even though America, in the past, had been slave owners and slaves, they could lay that aside and become friends. He dreamt of seeing Americans not judged by color but by the individual character of a person, and that justice and equality would be available for all races of this great nation.

You may not have liked Dr. Martin Luther King, but you cannot deny that those words are words we should strive live by. Unlike today, his dream was equality for everybody, not just his race. His speech was so impactful that you can see it at the National Museum of African American History and Culture. If you have never heard the "I Have a Dream" speech, or haven't in a while, you can view him delivering that speech on YouTube. As a side note, He was a professed Christian. That could explain why he wanted people to be treated with respect and not harbor hate, and why, even though he was attacked with rocks, he didn't strike back.

Like the people who have taken Dr. Martin Luther King's dream and perverted it, the same goes true for Jude's dreamers. These dreamers do not have a dream that would make life easier or advance our ability to accomplish more, and their dream is not to bring unity to the body of Christ and our fellow man.

On the contrary, their dreams only bring satisfaction to themselves and their desires. They dreamed and had imaginations that consumed their thoughts, and they were not concerned with any adverse reactions that may come about because of their dreams. These people were the same as the people that the book of Genesis describes in chapter 6, verse five, *"And God saw that the wickedness of man was great in the earth, and that every imagination of the thoughts of his heart was only evil continually."* No wonder Jude compared them to those who lived in and around Sodom.

They didn't only imagine these evil and corrupt things but also practiced them. All they thought about was satisfying the flesh and having pleasure. Their complete identity was found in what they imagined. So true are the words found in the first part of Proverbs 23:7, *"For as he thinketh in his heart, so is he..."* If you talk to someone long enough, you will find out who they are inwardly, because sooner or later, what consumes their mind will fill their heart and be revealed out of their mouth.

72

Jude gives three things that can be seen that will identify a "filthy" dreamer. The first is, *"they defile the flesh."* 1st Corinthians 3:16 states, *"Know ye not that ye are the temple of God, and that the Spirit of God dwelleth in you? If any man defile the temple of God, him shall God destroy; for the temple of God is holy, which temple ye are."*

So what does that mean? Of course, anything we put in our bodies that is not healthy will bring problems, but here it is mainly referring to a specific thing. The answer can be found in Acts 15:29, *"That ye abstain from meats offered to idols, and from blood, and from things strangled, and from fornication: from which if ye keep yourselves, ye shall do well. Fare ye well."* So here it is mainly talking about our bodies taking in meat that had been offered to idols and the blood of an animal.

But, I find something interesting in this Scripture as well. He mentions something that you don't actually swallow. He mentions fornication. How does that defile the body if you can't eat it. 1st Corinthians 6:18 give more insight on this, *"Flee fornication. Every sin that a man doeth is without the body; but he that committeth fornication sinneth against his own body."* Fornication, it says, is the only sin that comes against the body.

When a person commits fornication, they are actually worshipping the devil and have invited the devil to control them. That is why people addicted to pornography can't shake it off that easily. It is said that pornography is harder to quit than any substance known to man. Sexual immorality is one of the top in the list of sins that God judges harshly.

73

1st Corinthians 6:9, *"Know ye not that the unrighteous shall not inherit the kingdom of God? Be not deceived: neither fornicators, nor idolaters, nor adulterers, nor effeminate, nor abusers of themselves with mankind...."* And in Colossians 3:5, *"Mortify therefore your members which are upon the earth; fornication, uncleanness, inordinate affection, evil concupiscence, and covetousness, which is idolatry..."*

When we look at Numbers chapter 25, we see that God is so against eating meat offered to idols and fornication that He destroyed more of the people of Israel for committing those sins than He did when they worshipped the golden calf. So the next time you decide to look at porn on the computer and say, "Well, it's not really hurting anyone," you might want to think again!

Jude further revealed that they *"despised* (rejected) *dominion."* They hated anything and everything that would go against them doing what they desired. They refused to be under any kind of law or government that would restrict their passions and lust.

Paul tells us that we should live under these guidances that God has established. *"Let every soul be subject unto the higher powers. For there is no power but of God: the powers that be are ordained of God."* Romans 13:1. Daniel 2:20-21 shows that God is in control and is in authority, *"...And Daniel answered and said, Blessed be the name of God for ever and ever: for wisdom and might are his: And he changeth the times and the seasons: he removeth kings, and setteth up kings: he giveth wisdom unto the wise, and knowledge to them that know understanding..."*

74

All throughout the Bible, it shows that God has set up an order of authority for everyone to follow. Ephesians chapter 6 gives the rank of authority that God set up for the home. Children should be under the parents, wives under the husband, and slaves under the master. But that didn't leave anyone without authority, not even the husbands and masters. The whole list, including the masters and husbands, are to be under the authority and leadership of God.

We shouldn't obey authority if they come against God's sovereignty and rules. A prime example is in Acts 5:26-29, *"Then went the captain with the officers, and brought them without violence: for they feared the people, lest they should have been stoned. And when they had brought them, they set them before the council: and the high priest asked them, Saying, Did not we straitly command you that ye should not teach in this name? and, behold, ye have filled Jerusalem with your doctrine, and intend to bring this man's blood upon us. Then Peter and the other apostles answered and said, We ought to obey God rather than men."*

Finally, Jude moves on to those who *"speak evil of dignities."* These filthy dreamers came against not only the government and laws that would intervene but anything in the spiritual realm, be it God, the law of Moses, or even what Christ taught. Remember, these people, according to Jude, were in the church. Can you see why Jude was coming against this so strongly?

Isaiah chapter 5:20 gives a harsh warning against people that speak against God, things holy, and don't respect authority, *"Woe unto them that call evil good, and good evil;*

that put darkness for light, and light for darkness; that put bitter for sweet, and sweet for bitter!" Just before that, in verse 14, Isaiah mentions that Hell has enlarged itself to accommodate these people. For the record, Isaiah was talking about God's people.

Listen up!!! God won't allow His people to live any way they please without judgment coming. I know I have said that before, but it's worth mentioning over and over. *"Be not deceived; God is not mocked: for whatsoever a man soweth, that shall he also reap. For he that soweth to his flesh shall of the flesh reap corruption; but he that soweth to the Spirit shall of the Spirit reap life everlasting."* Galatians 6:7-8.

I find it shocking that these bold, ungodly people could have been in the church unaware. But the truth is that man is bent toward sin in his natural state. Man is always trying to find a way to get around God's law and twist His Word for his own benefit. It was no different in the days of Jude.

Many false teachers came from the church. Some examples are the Simonians, who said that idolatry was not good or evil. They felt that all sex was to be considered perfect love. Their lives were utterly immoral, yet they thought themselves right with God.

Another group was the Nicolaitanes. God said in Revelation 2:6 that He hated them. They considered themselves Christians but taught people that the Lord Jesus Christ had hatred in His heart. Isn't it funny that even today, when we come against sin, we are called "haters?" The Nicolaitanes also abandoned the true Christian doctrine so they could live a life of self-indulgence.

Their name in the Hebrew language meant "destruction of people." That was a fitting name because what they were doing was trying to lead good Christians astray. Compare them to how Satan is described, *" Be sober, be vigilant; because your adversary the devil, as a roaring lion, walketh about, seeking whom he may devour…"* 1st Peter 5:8.

The common goal is to conquer and destroy anything that is pure and holy. They also used Christian liberty as the basis for them to freely obey the lust of the flesh and eat sacrifices given to idols. The Carpocratians practiced all of this but still used pictures of Jesus Christ as if they were followers of Him.

Paul wrote against using grace as a license to sin. Romans 6:1-2, 15. *"What shall we say then? Shall we continue in sin, that grace may abound? God forbid. How shall we, that are dead to sin, live any longer therein?… What then? Shall we sin, because we are not under the law, but under grace? God forbid."* In Romans chapter 8, when Paul talked about Jews living under the Law and Christians under grace, he showed that people were taking that to mean Christians could sin and get away with it. However, in verse 8 of Chapter 3, he says, *"And not rather, (as we be slanderously reported, and as some affirm that we say,) Let us do evil, that good may come? Whose damnation is just."*

Nowhere in the Scriptures, when taken in context, can anyone ever conclude that God is okay with sin. If you are a Christian practicing sin, you will face judgment. You might not die and go to hell, but rest assured you will be judged.

In verse 9, Jude gives an example of how Michael reacted to another spiritual entity. The model stemmed from an event that was recorded in Deuteronomy 34:5-6, *"So Moses the servant of the LORD died there in the land of Moab, according to the word of the LORD. And he buried him in a valley in the land of Moab, over against Bethpeor: but no man knoweth of his sepulchre unto this day."*

The full details of this event are not given in Deuteronomy or any other place in the Bible; it is only mentioned here in Jude. However, it begs to be noted that another apocryphal book called "The Assumption of Moses" contained the story as well, according to Origen, an early Christian scholar and theologian. That book since then is now lost.

Michael is called an archangel in the Scriptures and is the only angel in the Bible given that title. Michael in Greek means "judgment of blasphemy or evil-speaking." So obviously, he was a mighty angel with much authority.

Notice the wording in verse 6, *"And he...."* Many take that to mean the Lord Himself buried Moses because "Lord" was mentioned just before verse 6. Others view this to mean that the Lord watched over the burial, but Michael was actually the one who took the body and buried it. No matter which is correct, the point of the text is that Moses was buried in a place where no earthy man knew where it was.

Most commentaries and scholars believe it was essential to hide the body of Moses because the Jews were notorious for idol worship. They believe that if Satan could have exposed where the body of Moses was, Satan could get them to worship the body of Moses. Others think that the devil might have even possessed the body, making it appear alive, to influence the people further to make Moses an idol if he could have gotten to the body.

The point Jude was getting to had not so much to do with the body of Moses but with how Michael confronted Satan. Jude had just mentioned how these evil people had no respect for authority, either earthly or heavenly. But we see here that even in the spiritual realm, there is respect for people in power.

Many commentaries reference the *"railing accusation"* mentioned by Jude, means Michael did not want or didn't have the position to bring some judgment on Satan but that the Lord would bring that judgment. But I see a different and deeper meaning in this verse.

We already know that it is God that puts people in positions, as we learn from Romans 13:1. Often, it is hard for us to understand that even evil rulers had been placed in position by God. But, if they were put in authority, it was to bring about something that God wanted to be done. And God commanded us to honor that position.

We already know that Satan was in one of the top positions in Heaven, next to the Trinity. And, when he lost that position, God still made him ruler over the earth. That being said, when the Bible talks about the earth in these verses, it is to be understood that it is the worldly earth system, not the authority of the planet and all the inhabitants itself; God is still in control of ALL.

It does seem that there are two top authorities in the spirit realm, there is the Godhead, and there is Satan. It further appears that the only thing Satan has to honor is the Godhead. It doesn't appear that there is any other being over him except God.

As mentioned, Romans 13 plainly tells us that we are to honor the authorities that have been placed over us, and yes, that means even the bad ones. I hear people all the time saying, "That's not my president," when the one they didn't vote for lost. But whether you like it or not, once a President has been elected in our country, they are your president for that term of office.

Because God has placed them in that position, we are in the wrong if we talk badly about them. God "commanded" us to honor them and pray for them. The Bible even further reminds us that if we are a slave to someone, we are to honor the person over us as well.

When it came to this confrontation of Michael coming against Satan, the important thing I want you to see is how Michael addressed Satan. Michael said, *"The Lord rebuke thee."* That is an important lesson we all should learn. When confronting the devil, I hear people say **I** come against the power of darkness. **I** rebuke any evil force that is surrounding my life and family. **I** rebuke the spirit of poverty.

The problem is they are coming against these principalities in their own name. Satan and his demons have no fear when that happens and probably laugh. Only in the name of Jesus

Christ, can we come against any of the evil principalities in the world today. To go against them with your own power is not only foolish but dangerous. We all need to walk in the authority that Christ has given, obey the leaders that God has set over us, and call on God to intervene when needed.

Chapter 7

Ignorance is Not Bliss

"But these speak evil of those things which they know not: but what they know naturally, as brute beasts, in those things they corrupt themselves. Woe unto them! for they have gone in the way of Cain, and ran greedily after the error of Balaam for reward, and perished in the gainsaying of Core. Jude verses 10-11.

Jude, describing these people who have crept into the church, explains why they talk against God, against authority, and can do things that eventually will harm themselves. It's because they are blinded to spiritual things. 1st Corinthians 2:14 worded it this way, *"But the natural man receiveth not the things of the Spirit of God: for they are foolishness unto him: neither can he know them, because they are spiritually discerned."*

Ephesians 4:17-19 goes more into detail as to why wicked men do wicked things, *"This I say therefore, and testify in the Lord, that ye henceforth walk not as other Gentiles walk, in the vanity of their mind, Having the understanding darkened, being alienated from the life of God through the ignorance that is in them, because of the blindness of their heart: Who being past feeling have given themselves over unto lasciviousness, to work all uncleanness with greediness."*

Through man's pride and the desires of his heart, he turns away from the truth of God. When he continues to do this, he loses the ability to understand right from wrong. Jeremiah 17:9 exposes the truth about man's heart, *"The heart is deceitful above all things, and desperately wicked: who can know it?"*

Paul goes on to reveal that when we walk in the flesh, the flesh will come against God. Romans 8:6-7, *"For to be carnally minded is death; but to be spiritually minded is life and peace. Because the carnal mind is enmity against God: for it is not subject to the law of God, neither indeed can be."*

The people that Jude is referring to have intentionally turned against God. They have sold themselves to self-pleasure to the point that they no longer feel any regret or shame for their behavior. This is why Jude says they only know what comes naturally *"as brute beasts."*

They act like an animal, having no conscience or wisdom. Their knowledge is confined to sensual indulgence and things that will corrupt or destroy them.

The Bible uses several animals to describe man's behavior when he is in this condition. In Matthew 7:6, Jesus said, *"Give not that which is holy unto the dogs, neither cast ye your pearls before swine, lest they trample them under their feet, and turn again and rend you."* And in Revelation 22:15, *"For without are dogs, and sorcerers, and whoremongers, and murderers, and idolaters, and whosoever loveth and maketh a lie."* These verses show mankind in his filthiness and uncleanness.

Jesus in Matthew 10:16 says, *"Behold, I send you forth as sheep in the midst of wolves: be ye therefore wise as serpents, and harmless as doves."* When dealing with wolves, they always come in a pack, and they will attack an animal not only for food but also will kill them for no apparent reason. They always look for the weakest in the bunch and separate them from the rest.

Man, without God, is like a wild animal. He is ruthless, careless, fearless, harmful, dangerous, without a conscience or pity, immoral, self-centered, wasteful, and unknowing of his surroundings. He will take advantage of the weak and can't be trusted. It is all the same characteristic of the one they serve, Satan himself.

In verse 11, Jude sounds the alarm, *"Woe unto them."* The word "woe" here in Greek means "a primary exclamation of grief." It is the mark of terrible judgment or death. Jude is stressing the danger that these people are facing. It would be like a mother screaming at her child about to run in front of a car. It is a cry that demands immediate action to prevent an oncoming doom.

This type of woe is the same type found in Revelation 8:13. There, the woe is so resounding that heaven is silent for about half an hour. At that time, it is no use repenting and listening to the warning, for God is going to send His judgment on fallen man like never before in history. God has run out of patience for them. In Jude, there is still time to repent. When God sends us a warning, we should immediately heed that warning to prevent a disastrous calamity from befalling us. Unfortunately, the people Jude was referring to didn't and will receive their proper judgment.

Jude once again gives three descriptions of how they erred. Each opens up information about why judgment is heading to these false teachers.

The first is, *"for they have gone in the way of Cain."* What is the significance of that? First, the way of Cain can be interpreted as how these false teachers were led. They started down the path because, in the beginning, they didn't understand the Scriptures and were being taught wrong. Genesis chapter 4 further explains why going after the way of Cain was terrible.

The story refers to when Cain and Able brought a sacrifice to God. It is believed that the day they did so was the same day when the Passover sacrifice would be made in the future. God wanted a blood offering; instead, Cain wanted to present an offering to God by giving Him something he had toiled to bring. So, in other words, Cain was trying to contribute works to cover his debt to God, but as we know now, works will never redeem us or satisfy God.

Notice also in Genesis 4:3-4, *"And in process of time it came to pass, that Cain brought of the fruit of the ground an offering unto the LORD. And Abel, he also brought of the firstlings of his flock and of the fat thereof. And the LORD had respect unto Abel and to his offering..."* Notice something interesting? It doesn't mention that Cain even gave his first fruit; however, Abel gave the first and best to God as God commanded.

Verse 5 of Genesis, chapter 4, tells us that God not only didn't have respect for Cain's offering but didn't have respect for Cain either. God wasn't happy with what Cain had done. Because of this, Cain became wroth (very angry).

In verse 7, God tries to instruct Cain on the way he should go and why God wasn't happy, *"If thou doest well, shalt thou not be accepted? And if thou doest not well, sin lieth at the door. And unto thee shall be his desire, and thou shalt rule over him."*

However, the heart of Cain was revealed. Instead of listening to God and repenting, he resisted the correction and killed his brother. He wanted to remove the bar that Abel had set. Furthermore, when asked about his brother by God, Cain showed no concern for his brother and even lied to God. See that path that sin will carry you when you resist the correction of God?

God understands that mankind will fail from time to time. When we do, we need to repent to God. God wants us to have fellowship with Him and be obedient. He doesn't want to have to bring judgment. He would rather mend the relationship that has been broken.

To prove this, God said in Isaiah 1:18, *"Come now, and let us reason together, saith the LORD: though your sins be as scarlet, they shall be as white as snow; though they be red like crimson, they shall be as wool."* There is no need to be angry with God. There is no need to try and hide our sinful condition. God is willing and longing to forgive if we will but allow Him to.

Another path these false teachers traveled on was they *"ran greedily after the error of Balaam for reward."* Balaam was an interesting character in the Bible. According to Joshua 13:22, Balaam was the son of Beor and also a soothsayer, which seems to mean he used divination to get answers for people.

The setting Jude refers to here is found in Numbers chapter 22. The story surrounds two main characters, Balaam and Balak. Balak was a Moabitish King. Israel had already done mighty works against the Amorites. Balak knew this; therefore, when he saw the Israelites pitching their tents on the plains of Moab, he became afraid that Israel was going to take him over as well.

It is apparent that Balaam's power was well known abroad because Balak sent messengers to him. Balaam was around 420 miles from where Balak was. I am sure that he could have found other soothsayers to get an answer for his case, or I'm sure he could have gotten help from surrounding armies, but something is said in the message that reveals why he wanted Balaam to intervene.

Look at it with me, *"Come now therefore, I pray thee, curse me this people; for they are too mighty for me: peradventure I shall prevail, that we may smite them, and that I may drive them out of the land: for I wot that he whom thou blessest is blessed, and he whom thou cursest is cursed."* Numbers 22:6. Do you see it?! *"for I wot* (am certain) *that he whom thou blessest is blessed, and he whom thou cursest is cursed."* Obviously, Balaam's power was stronger than probably anyone else's.

It is almost ironic that Balak is asking Balaam, a soothsayer, to curse the people of Israel. I believe I have read in the Bible somewhere that would bring a curse on anyone that comes against Israel, *"And I will bless them that bless thee* (speaking of Israel), *and curse him that curseth thee: and in thee shall all families of the earth be blessed."* Genesis 12:3.

If Balak believes that Balaam can curse the people of God, then he clearly doesn't understand the power and might of God. He and the others around him believed so much in the power of Balaam that they brought money to encourage Balaam to do the deed.

The next few verses give the account of what happened after Balaam had received the message. Balaam told the messengers that he would have to consult "the Lord" and would let them know what the Lord said.

I wouldn't think it so strange that Balaam, although a soothsayer, would ask the Lord what to do. Why? Because even Satan knows that God is above all and in charge of all. That was proven when Satan wanted to attack Job. He could only go as far as God would allow him to. Even today's witches and warlocks, when interviewed, say that they have NO POWER over the children of God. That should give you great comfort if you are a believer in Jesus Christ.

Sure enough, in verse 12, God told Balaam not to curse Israel, for they are blessed. But that didn't stop Balak from trying again. This time he sent more honorable messengers to state that he would give Balaam whatever he wanted if he would just curse the children of Israel.

Balaam again refused the offer saying even if they gave him a house full of silver and gold, he couldn't go beyond the Word of the Lord, but this time added, "my God."

Although Balaam in word claimed God was his God, his actions showed otherwise. God had already told him not to go and curse the people, but Balaam again asked God for permission. This time God told Balaam if they asked him to go, then go with them.

This, on the surface, seems that God may have changed His mind. But in reality, God knew that Balaam's heart and desire were for the promised riches, and he had no desire to do what God wanted him to do, so He allowed Balaam to make the decision whether to follow God's commandment or not.

Because of his greed, Balaam decided to go with Balak after all. Balaam was nothing more than lip service to God. Many people say that God is their Lord, but their lives prove otherwise.

Because Balaam disobeyed God's commandment, he was confronted on the journey by an angel whose intent was to kill Balaam before he could do anything to the children of Israel. The story of this event has been known to most people of faith since childhood. It is the story where the donkey spoke. You can read all the details in Numbers chapter 22. The bottom line, God opened Balaam's eyes and gave him one more chance to repent. This time he did.

Oh, if the story just ended there. Unfortunately, Balaam continued to try and butter God up to get his way by offering sacrifices on altars. He was trying to change God's mind so that he could get what his heart still desired, even after being given a second chance at life.

Revelation reveals the plan that Balaam eventually made for Balak that would come out to be more destructive to the people of Isreal than anything before and possible after. Revelation 2:14, *"But I have a few things against thee, because thou hast there them that hold the doctrine of Balaam, who taught Balac to cast a stumblingblock before the children of Israel, to eat things sacrificed unto idols, and to commit fornication."*

Balaam not only sinned but caused a whole nation to sin. The things you do in life in front of people can either lead them to God or away from Him. The thing Balaam did by turning the Israelites away from God eventually cost him his life. Love of money, power, and fame can destroy not only your life but all those around you.

Finally, we reach the story of Core (Korah). The complete details are found in Numbers chapter 16. In this story, Korah stirred people to come against Moses and his authority over the people. And as usual, misery loves company, so he convinced 250 highly respected people in the congregation to do likewise.

Korah didn't want to obey and follow Moses and Aaron anymore. He felt that they had led them into the wilderness to die. Korah twisted the Word of God and made these people believe that all of them were holy and just as capable of being priests and making atonement for the people of Israel.

Korah didn't understand that when Moses spoke, he was speaking what God had told him. So, in essence, Korah wasn't coming against Moses; he was coming against God Himself. Korah felt Moses and Aaron had lifted themselves above the people and given themselves power.

Of course, when Korah made these accusations, he did it in a way to make it look like he wanted to take the burden of all the work Moses did and let them share it. But had Korah understood how God had set up the authority over the people, he would have known that he was not qualified.

When Moses heard what Korah had said, he immediately fell upon his face. Moses knew that God was a jealous God and wouldn't tolerate blasphemous statements such as this. It was, as I said, not so much that Korah spoke against Moses and Aaron but against God and His plan.

I see people in the church today talking against the headship. They judge against the chosen people of God who are called to lead the flock and speak to people behind their backs, telling how they would run things if they were in power or how wrong the leaders are.

They try to stir up the people and convince them that they need to get a new leader. If God truly sends the person they are talking about to lead the people, they have placed themselves in a dangerous position by talking about them.

Psalms 105:15 makes it very clear that a person shouldn't come against anyone that is anointed, *"Saying, Touch not mine anointed, and do my prophets no harm."* The word anointed means to be set apart in this verse. So, God is warning people not to come against leaders of the flock or anyone that has been set apart for the work of God. To me, this would even be the little old woman that cleans the toilet in the church if that is what God set her apart to do.

God's wrath arose, and because of what Korah did, God told Moses to get the congregation away from Korah and his people and belongings. God then opened the earth and swallowed Korah, the 250 people, and their belongings. How true the statement is in Hebrews 10:31, *"It is a fearful thing to fall into the hands of the living God."*

The people that God told to stay away from those wicked men were spared. However, the problem was that many of the congregation was still swayed by the words that Korah said. They, too, believed that Moses and Aaron were in the wrong. This is why we can't allow discord to come into the church.

Because the people came against Moses and Aaron, God's wrath once again arose, and He began to hit the people with a plague. God would have taken out the whole congregation if Moses hadn't intervened, but because Moses stood in the gap, most were spared. The total of those that died from the plague was fourteen thousand and seven hundred, besides them that died about the matter of Korah.

What a tragic story. Yet, in the church during Jude's day were people like Korah who had opposed God's appointed messengers and God's Son whom God had set over the church.

When Jude said, *"and perished in the gainsaying of Core,"* it means that people who have this kind of behavior are as good as dead if they don't repent. Believe it or not, they are still those in the church today rebelling against God's authority as Korah did. They, too, if they don't repent, will face the wrath of God. I beg of you, be careful how you talk about God's people!

So, to recap, the woe that Jude is sternly warning about deals mainly with these three aspects. First, going the way of Cain, or people being deceived into thinking that we don't have to do it God's way. That God will be okay with any type of service and life we want to give him.

The ten commandments are NOT suggestions; they are COMMANDMENTS. If God has said He wants things done a certain way, He means it. And like Cain, if God demands that we come to Him only by the sacrifice His Son Jesus Christ provided, then there is no other way you can get there to Heaven than that.

Through the teaching of people who revered education over the leading of the Holy Spirit, these people drifted from the true Word of God and became a hindrance to the church as well as set for themselves damnation. Colossians 2:8 warns, *"Beware lest any man spoil you through philosophy and vain deceit, after the tradition of men, after the rudiments of the world, and not after Christ."* Keep your eyes on Jesus, stay in His Word for direction, and lean on the

Holy Spirit as your guide to avoid falling like these false prophets.

The second are people who, even after being shed such mercy and grace, still return to their old sinful ways because of the love of money or this world.

Demas is a perfect example of this in the New Testament. In Philemon 1:24, he is listed as one of Paul's very own fellow laborers. He had walked and worked beside one of the most, if not the most, important missionary figures in our Bible. We also find him in Colossians 4:14, working beside the "beloved physician John," and obviously knew Luke.

Surely he was doing the work of the Lord. Surely he was committed to the Lord's service, yet in 2nd Timothy 4:10, Paul says, *"For Demas hath forsaken me, having loved this present world, and is departed unto Thessalonica; Crescens to Galatia, Titus unto Dalmatia."* From the way Paul had written this letter, others also walked with him and returned to the world's system.

Finally, he mentions people like Core (Korah) who do not want to listen to preachers, teachers, or any other authority. They want to do as they please and not be bothered. Their motto is whatever feels good, do it.

But, as Christians, we can not be this way. We have to remember what Paul wrote, *"What? know ye not that your body is the temple of the Holy Ghost which is in you, which ye have of God, and ye are not your own? For ye are bought with a price: therefore glorify God in your body, and in your spirit, which are God's."* 1st Corinthians 6:19-20.

These all fall with the same temptations that Satan uses on everyone, even when he was tempting Christ, *"Love not the world, neither the things that are in the world. If any man love the world, the love of the Father is not in him. For all that is in the world, the lust of the flesh, and the lust of the eyes, and the pride of life, is not of the Father, but is of the world."* 1st John 2:15-16.

Are there other sins that God will send harsh judgment on? Of course, but the origin of those sins, other than the ones mentioned above, falls under the same three things which cause a person to rebel and sin against God in the first place, *"...the lust of the flesh, and the lust of the eyes, and the pride of life..."*

Be watchful *"...because your adversary the devil, as a roaring lion, walketh about, seeking whom he may devour..."* 1st Peter 5:8. It is not the secular world that Satan is after; it is the Christian, God's people. Just because you have been given the grace and mercy of the Lord does not exempt you from falling away from the faith. So we need to do as Paul said at the beginning of verse 8, *"Be sober, be vigilan..."*

Chapter 8

All That Glitters Isn't Gold

"These are spots in your feasts of charity, when they feast with you, feeding themselves without fear: clouds they are without water, carried about of winds; trees whose fruit withereth, without fruit, twice dead, plucked up by the roots; Raging waves of the sea, foaming out their own shame; wandering stars, to whom is reserved the blackness of darkness for ever." Jude verses 12-13.

Jude now begins to show the destructive characters of these false prophets. What we do in secret will always sooner or later be revealed in the open. Jude says to begin with, *"These are spots in your feasts of charity."*

There are a couple of things we must know before going further. The first thing is the word "spots" actually means properly, "a rock by or in the sea, or cliffs. The rock can either be by the sea, where boats may be wrecked, or hidden in the sea, which means they could be stranded at any time unexpectedly. The analogy here is that the hidden truth about what these false teachers believed and taught could cause a person to shipwreck their faith. They were as dangerous in the church as hidden rocks to mariners in the ocean.

We have a story in history that gives a perfect example of that. It is the Titanic. The Titanic was said to be unsinkable, and they had no fear of rocks or anything else the ocean had in it, but sadly, the ship sank because of an iceberg, and the majority of people on that ship died in the cold waters of night. Christians can sink into utter despair if they are not watchful and may never recover here on this earth.

The second thing to notice is that the word "feast" has been added to the text. The word "charity" used here is for love but is in the plural form. There was no known "feast" of love in the Bible or the Jewish teachings. This phrase Jude uses seems to take on the meaning of a time of fellowship that believers share among themselves for strengthening, encouraging, and leaning on each other for support, kind of like we do when we gather for church or Sunday School.

The Bible warns us that as the end of time draws near, we should spend more time with other believers, *"And let us consider one another to provoke unto love and to good works: Not forsaking the assembling of ourselves together, as the manner of some is; but exhorting one another: and so much the more, as ye see the day approaching."* Hebrews 10:24-25. We can see how hard it is to live a Christian life today. It is only going to get worse, and it will soon be vital that we spend time together in order to stay faithful.

I personally believe it is almost impossible to live a healthy, victorious Christian life and not have fellowship with other believers. There are times in our lives when we need someone to talk to when things are getting tough. We need others to speak wisdom into our lives through the Scriptures when Satan is trying to make us doubt, give up, or question what God has said. We need to know we are not alone in the faith. And Lord knows we need to be there to give our tithes and offerings to help the church accomplish all that needs to be done.

Not only do we need to draw from others through fellowship, but we ourselves need to be used to help others in their times of need like others do for us. This is what these false teachers wanted NO part of. Jude shows this in the following statement; *"when they feast with you, feeding themselves without fear..."* They only want what they can get. They have no desire to help or encourage anyone but themselves. Their motto is, "my name is Jimmy, and I'll take all you gimme."

Not only in the area of Christian fellowship, but these false teachers were taking advantage of holy things like the Lord's Supper and turning it into an ordinary feast. When Jude says *"without fear,"* it means they had no reverence toward God or what these things stood for. They were there just to feed their bellies, to get a free buffet, so to speak.

The next similitude Jude uses is, *"clouds they are without water."* According to Judaism, rain is a type of blessing. *"Then shall we know, if we follow on to know the LORD: his going forth is prepared as the morning; and he shall come unto us as the rain, as the latter and former rain unto the earth."* Hosea 6:3. Hosea is talking about how God will bring His people back to their land and bless them in the future. Jude is trying to say once again that these people can't bring any type of blessing because they are all concerned with being blessed.

But there is more to rain than just being a blessing. Rain is vital to bring water to sustain life all over the world. Man can live almost one hundred days without food, but he can only survive for three days without water. God used the rain in times past to bring judgment through the flood and to show He has full control of everything, as He showed in the stories recorded in Genesis chapter 47 and in 1st Kings chapter 18, to give a couple of examples.

Rain also brings growth. Without rain, plants, trees, fruit, vegetables, and everything on earth would wither and die. The Holy Spirit is represented as living water. As believers, we are to be so filled with this living water that it spreads to others.

John 7:37-38 says, *"In the last day, that great day of the feast, Jesus stood and cried, saying, If any man thirst, let him come unto me, and drink. He that believeth on me, as the scripture hath said, out of his belly shall flow rivers of living water."* The Holy Spirit wants to use us to bring people to the river of life, Jesus Christ. People can see or be touched by the Holy Spirit through physical contact, observing our behavior, or what we say. We are clouds that God uses to help bring that life-giving water to others.

But the only way for that to happen is that we must be filled with the Holy Spirit. Obviously, these false teachers were not filled with the Holy Spirit, so they could not give the life-giving substance that people need to live both physically on this earth and eternally after death. Are you supplying the life-giving waters to those around you?

These false prophets are also paralleled by *"trees whose fruit withereth, without fruit."* Everyone knows that a tree will begin to produce fruit during the spring, and the fruit starts to wither away by fall.

There are several reasons a tree might not bear fruit naturally. One is not being adequately graphed; another is that the atmosphere might be too cold. The tree may not get enough water to supply the fruit or fertilizer to give it the proper nutrients. The spacing might not be far away enough for it to bear fruit. Or maybe it is not getting enough sun for it to grow correctly. And to maintain good fruit, the tree must have pollination and be pruned.

Fruit is needful for the body, and it protects from diseases that attack the body, helps get rid of harmful waste, and supplies vital nutrients to the body. With all that being said, now let's go back to the analogy of these false prophets not having fruit and what the cause might be along with the result.

The first thing I mentioned is that to get good fruit, the tree must be grafted by a good line of fruit trees. There are different types of fruit, but to produce fruit with high quality, taste, and benefits, you must start with a tree that has all of those qualities in the beginning. Just planting any seed will not produce an excellent fruit-bearing tree.

A good tree stock used to graft other trees is valuable and highly treasured. For believers to produce high-quality fruit, we must be grafted into a high-quality, highly valued family tree. This is none other than our Lord and Savior, Jesus Christ. Romans 11:24 gives a good example of this, *"For if thou wert cut out of the olive tree which is wild by nature, and wert grafted contrary to nature into a good olive tree: how much more shall these, which be the natural branches, be grafted into their own olive tree?"* We need to be removed from our old family tree and placed in God's family tree to produce the fruit that will change people's lives. It is not us but what flows through us by the excellent stock we are graphed into.

If a believer is cold or indifferent, they will not bear good fruit. A person, like a tree, gets cold when they are not near enough to the sun. In the Christian sense, it is the Son, not the sun. For us as Christians to be effective, we must have a daily connection with the Lord and the Holy Spirit to warm our souls and keep the fire burning within us. The further we get from that, the colder this old heart will become. For non-believers, they have had no connection with the Son. Thus, they are not only cold; they are dead cold and will never produce any kind of fruit that will benefit them or anyone else. This is probably the case with the false prophets.

To me, the water and fertilizer needed to produce a healthy bearing fruit tree is the filling of the Holy Spirit and the Word of God. If a believer doesn't have enough of either, they don't have enough energy and provision for sharing with others. They're spending all of their time just trying to survive. By what Jude is describing, these false prophets are not filled with the Spirit of God and are twisting the only little knowledge they have of the Word of God.

Trees must be separated far enough so that the other trees don't hinder the growth of the other. As believers, we are commanded to be separated from this world. If we live our lives the same as the world, we are no benefit to God's kingdom and will not produce good fruit. We must separate ourselves from the world, but we also need to minister to them. It takes the power of the Holy Spirit to help us not to conform to the world as we do this. The false prophets probably have never been separated from the world by accepting the Lord Jesus Christ as their Savior in the first place.

A tree will need to be pruned from time to time to produce good fruit. When a branch on the tree becomes unproductive, it hinders the whole tree from being productive. In comparison, the Christian must remove any of the branches that are causing the tree from producing. It might be that we are spending too much time watching television, or it could be too much focus on our hobby, or worse, we have something evil in our lives.

Anything that takes away from God's work must be cut out of our lives if we expect to be a good fruit bearer for Christ. This doesn't mean that we don't live a life of our own, but it does require that we devote the proper time to God's work and keep ourselves clean.

One of the biggest keys for a fruit tree to produce is pollination. In order to do this, there must be at least two trees for fruit, one male and one female. Christ is compared to being the husband to the bride (the church). The only way to produce fruit is through our relationship with Christ. We can't produce fruit in our own power. Most likely, the reason these false prophets are described by Jude as a tree with no fruit is that they have never had a relationship with Christ. John 15:5 states, *"I am the vine, ye are the branches: He that abideth in me, and I in him, the same bringeth forth much fruit: for without me ye can do nothing."*

The fruit we bear should help protect people and ourselves, help get rid of the waste this world produces in us and others, and provide the needful benefits to help us live day by day.

Every Christian should be producing fruit. If you are not, there is something wrong, and you need to ask the Holy Spirit what your spiritual tree needs in order to produce fruit. If we want to show the glory of God to the world, we must bear fruit. John 15:8, *"Herein is my Father glorified, that ye bear much fruit; so shall ye be my disciples."*

In closing on this subject, I would also like to say there is timing involved. Just as a tree needs time to grow older and also has seasons it must go through to produce fruit, so it is with a Christian. We can't expect newborn Christians to go out without helping them become strong in the Word and their faith, and we can't push fruit production in our power.

We, too, have seasons we need to go through; times of growth, prosperity and production, and times when we will become weak and need God to bring us back to life. It is all done by the power and timing of God.

Jude describes these false prophets as *"twice dead."* Most likely, this refers to the fact that they are not only going to die a physical death, but they are also spiritually dead. It is very probable that they have never been saved by the grace of God in the first place.

Finally, he concludes with them being *"plucked up by the roots."* Matthew 13:5-6, talking about the seed of God's Word, describes how this happens, *"Some fell upon stony places, where they had not much earth: and forthwith they sprung up, because they had no deepness of earth: And when the sun was up, they were scorched; and because they had no root, they withered away."*

Whether these false prophets knew God or not, they were not rooted in Him, and when the pressures of the world came, they became ineffective. We must put our total trust in God's Word, firmly established in the faith, if we are to make it in this world and produce fruit so others can become fruit bearers.

These false prophets are also described as *"raging waves of the sea, foaming out their own shame…"* Isaiah uses this great metaphor in chapter 57:20, *"But the wicked are like the troubled sea, when it cannot rest, whose waters cast up mire and dirt."* The description can be seen as how the sea is in a storm, and the sea creates great swells that crash against the shore, making a deafening sound. While doing so, it stirs up the muddy, putrid sediments from the ocean and pours them upon the sands of the beach.

Just like the sea's actions, these people were proud and arrogant. They were headstrong and unruly. They made a lot of noise in stirring up their beliefs and passions. Like the sea, they were inconstant as water in the ocean, turbulent and restless. They couldn't cease the sins they committed. Because of their frequent and irregular changes, they were unfaithful and undependable.

The word "shame" here is used in a plural form. It suggests a continuing type of shame. The result was a constant shame that they didn't mind people seeing, not only a shame to them but a shame on the body of Christ. This brought more harm than good to the body of Christ.

Then Jude says they were like *"wandering stars."* The Bible tells us that the stars were made for signs and seasons in Genesis. Stars are often used to navigate people at night. Seamen use the stars to guide their vessels when they have no other means to do so.

Unlike normal stars and planets, which have a direct path that can be counted on, these stars are more like a meteor with no clear path to follow or that can be counted on, much less followed. Also, like a meteor, often they come in as a blaze, ready to do it all, and then fizzle out in the darkness, never to be seen again. These people will misdirect and deceive others in their path.

Like so many other types of people Jude has mentioned, these will end up in total darkness, void of God. We, as believers, have been called to reflect the Light of the World. Christ is that light. Christ is dependable. You can count on Him to be faithful, never changing, and the guide you need to make it in your life journey.

Chapter 9

Judgement Day is Coming

"And Enoch also, the seventh from Adam, prophesied of these, saying, Behold, the Lord cometh with ten thousands of his saints, To execute judgment upon all, and to convince all that are ungodly among them of all their ungodly deeds which they have ungodly committed, and of all their hard speeches which ungodly sinners have spoken against him."
Jude verses 14-15.

Jude begins with this verse identifying the person he refers to as *"Enoch also, the seventh from Adam."* He wanted them to understand that this particular Enoch was the seventh from Adam. I believe he did this because, as stated before, many Jewish people understood their heritage and lineage very well. Most would have known that Cain also named a child of his Enoch.

It is essential not to confuse which Enoch, Jude is speaking about, unlike when he introduces his brother James at the beginning of his writing. When Jude mentioned he was the brother of James, it wasn't to focus on James, but he wanted more focus on Christ. But here, he wants no mistake in the identity of this person. Why? Because of what he said next; *"prophesied of these, saying..."*

Can you see now the importance? We have already gone over how Cain's life panned out. Usually, children take up the habits of their father. If Cain's child did, he wouldn't be one that I would expect to give a prophecy. However, when we look at Enoch being the seventh from Adam, there is not much information about him, but what is *found* is **profound**.

What is recorded in the Bible about Enoch is his father's name was Jared. We also know that Enoch was the father of Methuselah, who is said to have been the oldest person that has ever lived. We know that Enoch lived to be three hundred and sixty-five years old. We also know that Enoch was Noah's great-grandfather, the same Noah whom he and his family were spared from the great flood.

But the most important detail that I feel is recorded is in Genesis 5:24, "And Enoch walked with God: and he was not; for God took him." Enoch seemed so dear to God that God spared him from physical death but took him up to be with Him. Escaping death happened to only one other person besides Enoch, and that was Elijah, who God took up in a whirlwind, as recorded in 2nd Kings 2:1.

Many people believe Enoch and Elijah will be the two prophets slain during the great tribulation. Why? Because the Bible says, "… *it is appointed unto men once to die, but after this the judgment…*" Hebrews 9:27. If that be true that all men must face death one day, it could stand to reason these two still have that appointment to make. But still, we can't be dogmatic in that belief; it is totally up to God who these two will be.

The statement *"Behold, the Lord cometh with ten thousands of his saints"* many believe is a reference Jude used from Daniel 7:10, which states, *"A fiery stream issued and came forth from before him: thousand thousands ministered unto him, and ten thousand times ten thousand stood before him: the judgment was set, and the books were opened...* " But Jude specifically mentioned that it was Enoch that spoke the words. In order for Jude to say that, there must have either been some manuscripts preserved by Enoch or what Enoch had said was passed down from generation to generation. For your convenience, here is what is quoted in the book of Enoch, "Behold he comes with ten thousand of his saints, to execute judgment upon them, and destroy the wicked, and reprove all the carnal, for everything which the sinful and ungodly have done and committed against him..."

If you notice, I didn't italicize these words as I did with quotes from individuals and the holy Scriptures, and there is a reason for that, which I will explain later. But first, I want to go over a word Jude used to describe the statement that followed, which is "prophesied." When Jude used that word, it put weight on the spoken prophecy. How so? By using the word prophesied, he was actually stating that God inspired Enoch's words. Not only that, but the Old Testament gave strict guidelines and signs to look for when dealing with prophets. If a prophet didn't live up to that standard, they were to be stoned to death.

Peter also explains that prophecy only comes from the Holy Spirit and not from man, so if Enoch had prophesied this statement, he would fall into the category of a prophet. But then comes up the question of whether Jude had quoted from the book of Enoch in a couple of places in his writing. And if so, why do we not have a record of that book in our Bible today?

It may shock you, but over one hundred verses in the New Testament seem to have had their base from the book of Enoch or through Jewish tradition. Especially when dealing with resurrection, which the Sadducees didn't believe in but Jesus taught. One such comparison is found in Luke 20:34-36 compared to Enoch 15:1-7. Many also believe that when Jesus said in Mark 12:24-25, *"..., Do ye not therefore err, because ye know not the scriptures, neither the power of God? For when they shall rise from the dead, they neither marry, nor are given in marriage; but are as the angels which are in heaven,"* He, Christ, took that from the book of Enoch as well. They hold their opinion because to them, when Christ mentions Scriptures, the only ones that made a statement like that were from the book of Enoch. So, again, if all of this is true, why is the book of Enoch not in our Bible today?

I could write volumes of books to try to answer that question, so we will just hit the highlights. I suggest that if you want to know more about this subject, you spend quality time on an in-depth study and form your own opinion. That said, make sure you are using reliable information, not from sects or cults.

The first thing I want to bring up will probably shock most of the followers of the King James 1611 version of the Bible of which I am a follower. Did you know that at the beginning of the original King James 1611 version of the Bible, right in between the Old and New Testaments, there were 14 other, mostly partial books called the *"Apocrypha?"* By the way, the word "Apocrypha" means hidden.

When the original King James 1611 version of the Bible was written, these books were included along with maps and genealogies as well. All of this information stayed in that version of the Bible for 274 years before it was removed in 1885 A.D. Some portions of these books were called deuterocanonical books by some, such as the Catholic church.

Still, this doesn't answer why these writings are not in our Bible today, or for that matter, in the Hebrew Bible. There are many opinions on why. Some believe it is not in the Hebrew text because some of these writings refer to Christ as equal to God. To them, there is only one God, not a Trinity. Tertullian made this same argument for defending these books in the 2nd century to the church. I will give more details about Tertullian in a moment. Some people believe that it was taken out of the King James version because of the cost of printing.

Here are a few more reasons why it may be that they are not in our Bible today. Even though some believe that Christ and His disciples used portions of some of these books when they spoke, there is still no actual proof, as they never quoted where they were quoting from, with the exception of Jude, but even then, Jude is not a part of the Apocrypha.

Our Bibles today have many places where prophecies were given and fulfilled. In the Apocrypha, there is not one that has been fulfilled. Thus, our Bible is proven to be inspired by God since almost all the prophecies given have been fulfilled.

Some things strictly go contrary to our Bible. Some of the books, for instance, talk about prayer for the dead, purgatory, and against salvation through faith and faith alone because they teach you can obtain salvation through good works and giving.

Many of the Apocrypha books also contain errors in geographical details as well as historical ones. In the Bible we have today, we are still discovering just how accurate the facts contained are, and so far, nothing has been found on the contrary.

In our Bible today, we find many places with words like "and God said" or "the word of the Lord came unto me and said." There are no books in the Apocrypha that have statements like that. That makes it appear that God did not inspire the writers, or they would have at least said He spoke to them.

The Catholic church included the Apocrypha with the other sixty-six books of the Bible because Marin Luther accused them of using the Apocrypha instead of the sixty-six books. Hence, the Catholic Church accepted the Apocrypha as inspiration so they could continue to use the books. That all took place during the Protestant Reformation.

The reason Marin Luther came against it was for what was mentioned earlier. The Catholic church was using those books to justify their praying to the dead, and they wanted to continue to make money on its members, telling them that they could pay for their lost loved ones' way out of purgatory.

111

There is no known reason why the Apocrypha was placed in the King James 1611 version, but some speculate it was because most of the other Bibles of that time had it in theirs. However, almost all of them just had them added but said they didn't view them as being inspired or part of the sixty-six books that were deemed inspired.

Most also gave warning against adding them because of what Revelation 22:18 stated, *"For I testify unto every man that heareth the words of the prophecy of this book, If any man shall add unto these things, God shall add unto him the plagues that are written in this book..."* However, when reading that Scripture, it appears it is talking about the book of Revelation rather than the whole Bible.

Here is a quote from Marin Luther concerning the Apocrypha books, *"Apocrypha--that is, books which are not regarded as equal to the Holy Scriptures, and yet are profitable and good to read."*

I have to agree with that statement as well. Most of them were written on papyrus, which is parchment and copper, and mainly in Hebrew, Aramaic, Greek, and Nabataean-Aramaic. Some of these are dated before 70 A.D. With all the negatives I listed, I need to be fair and state that during the 2nd century, some of the early church fathers like Tertullian, Irenaeus, and Clement of Alexandra thought the book of Enoch to be Scripture.

In those Dead Sea Scrolls, there were also fragments of our biblical canon as well as an almost entire scroll of the book of Isaiah, which, interestingly enough, was almost word for word what is in our canon today. Once again, this is just to whet your appetite to dig deeper into the study of our Bible. The main reason I wanted to explain some of this is that we are talking about statements that may have come from the book of Enoch.

The book of Enoch was one of the portions of fragments that was found in the Dead Sea Scrolls. Enoch supposedly writes it. This has sparred big debates because most do not believe anything could have survived the flood; therefore, many do not think it is reliable and could be considered inspired.

That makes a good point, but playing the devil's advocate, you could also say that because Enoch was Noah's great-grandfather, Noah's family could have told stories to Noah about his great-grandfather, and from there, someone could have written what was said. I know that I never met my father's dad, but I know stories about him that were passed down from my father, aunts, and uncles. Because they knew him, I consider what they say to be true. It is to be noted that Tertullian made this same argument for defending the book in the 2nd century.

But there are other reasons to consider if the book of Enoch is inspired or not. We have already gone over verse six of Jude, where many believe the angels had relationships with earthly women causing them to sin and thus being cast out of their positions. People say that couldn't happen because all of the Bible centers around the sin of Adam and his bloodline, condemning us to death without the shed blood of Jesus Christ. They say that sin wouldn't be passed down if Adam wasn't the father. However, playing the devil's advocate again, corruption was still involved because the angels sinned in what they did, which would have also resulted in a sinful conception.

Then people argue that the book of Enoch certainly couldn't be taken as inspired because it records what many interpret as giants as tall as 442 feet coming from these illicit affairs of the angels and earthly women. I hate saying this, but playing the devil's advocate one more time, I would say there is also no way that, according to science, a whale could ever swallow a man, but tell that to Jonah! And as far as the giants being that tall, it never was fully understood what the word ells meant that Enoch mentioned when giving the height of these giants, so the measurement may not have been what the interpreters thought.

But let's say they got the measurement right. Let's look at a few more things that might justify what the book of Enoch said. We read in the story of the twelve spies sent out to scout the land of Canaan that ten came back and reported, *"And there we saw the giants, the sons of Anak, which come of the giants: and we were in our own sight as grasshoppers, and so we were in their sight."* Numbers 13:33.

Now, if the giants were over 400 feet and the average man in that day was around 5'6", wouldn't you think they would look like grasshoppers to the giants? Just maybe they were telling the truth. And to further establish that things in Canaan weren't like the rest of the areas, they brought back a cluster of grapes that took two men to carry. I would say it would take some mighty big hands to eat fruit that size.

But laying aside the devil's advocate act, there are many things in the book of Enoch and all the other fragments and books that were not a part of the canon that don't seem to fit in what we would call inspired Scripture. Furthermore, there is no way of telling who actually wrote these non-canon books or when. All that being said, this is why I didn't put the words coming from the book of Enoch in italics, because I can't say for sure that it can be trusted. But you can come to your own conclusion after your study.

With all this being said, here is my personal opinion. Although it may be intriguing to know what is in these other books that are not in our modern-day canon, I have complete confidence that the power of God, through the Holy Spirit moving on earthly man, has given us all we need to know in the canon we hold today. I will go further to say if you are not strong in your faith and doctrine, I wouldn't even bother reading those books.

The Bible we know has a central theme throughout every New and Old Testament page: God has made everything that is, and man is sinful by nature and needs a sacrifice to pay for that sin debt, or he will have to pay for it with his life. God is a holy God and demands holiness and perfection, which man himself can't do. That God, from the beginning, had made a plan by allowing His Son Jesus Christ to come and be that holy sacrifice for man, and if a man would believe and follow Christ, his sin debt would be paid. Our Bible confirms that Jesus Christ not only died but rose again to present that blood payment for sin to His Father. The Holy Spirit, part of the God-head, was then sent to earth to lead and guide the believers and draw the lost to Christ. The Bible explains throughout that this same Jesus Christ will return to call His children to Him and again to come back to earth to bring judgment on the lost and set up His millennial kingdom. Eventually, Satan and all the demons, along with their followers, will be cast away, a new heaven and earth will be created for all those who had put their trust in God, and forever we will be with Him where He is.

My friend, that is all we need to know and trust; the rest is like gravy on a biscuit. It doesn't matter who the sons of God were and if they did or did not have relationships with earthly women causing God to have to destroy the first earth by water. It doesn't matter about any other information within those other books that may or may not have happened. What matters is that we trust every inspired word in the Bible we hold in our hands today. Within those pages is more than we can handle now. Why would we need more?

So, to keep from dwelling on this, let's go to the last part of verse 14: "*Behold, the Lord cometh with ten thousands of his saints.*" When the Scripture says, "the Lord cometh," it actually states, "the Lord will come." The past tense is here used in prophetic style for the future to show the certainty of the event. In other words, you can take it to the bank that it will happen just as He said.

Regarding the saints mentioned, we today refer to saints as the saved, the born again, the redeemed ones, or Christians. But the original word applies to all holy, including the ones mentioned above and angels.

And why is He coming? *"To execute judgment upon all, and to convince all that are ungodly among them of all their ungodly deeds which they have ungodly committed, and of all their hard speeches which ungodly sinners have spoken against him."*

In the book of Jude, this verse is a continuation of verse 14, but the verses are combined in the book of Enoch. The ones that verse 15 is referring to will also be found in more detail in the succeeding verses.

If verse 14 had stopped there and didn't go on, all Christians could rejoice and say Hallelujah; Christ is coming! But unfortunately, it didn't stop there. On this occasion, He is not coming back to bring peace but judgment. The judgment referred to here is not the judgment God gave the world by the flood after Enoch, but rather this judgment is coming at the end of times for all sinners.

This type of judgment could only come about by a holy and righteous judge, which is why Christ is the one coming. He and He alone is the only one worthy to bring this type of judgment on mankind. The Lord God is good and merciful, but these verses remind people that though He is all of the above, He is also a just God and will not let sin run unchecked.

Many people today are trying to do away with preaching against sin and God's standards, but today, more than ever, even Christians need to hear that God will judge those who sin willfully.

117

To stress what Jude was saying and warning, he used two words repeatedly; they are ALL and UNGODLY. The first is, *"To execute judgment upon **all**."* Not one guilty person will be able to run or hide. He will find them and place judgment in their lives. Many people think they are hiding or getting away with sins because they are alone while doing them, but God is all-knowing and will bring that which is hidden into the light.

The next time all is mentioned is when he says, *"and to convince all that are ungodly among them of all their ungodly deeds which they have ungodly committed."* Here the word **convince** is not trying to prove that they are guilty but rather to **convict**, establish, reveal, or pronounce them as guilty. This is not as in our court system to establish guilt or not; this is the sentencing part.

And who is going to be convicted? "ALL that are UNGODLY." The first ungodly used here is to identify them, not just one but **all** of them. The word ungodly refers to not just mere sinners but the proud despisers of God. They have no fear of God or His judgments.

The next time ungodly is used, it is more of an adjective to describe their deeds, *"of **all** of their **ungodly** deeds."* What kind of deeds were they doing? Ungodly deeds. They were not doing anything to help others but wholly and fully living their lives to please themselves and their flesh.

Then he said, *"which they have **ungodly** committed."* This time the word ungodly is used as an adverb describing actions that they are doing. They can't blame anyone for their judgment but themselves. No one has forced them to sin; they have done it on their own accord.

The last ungodly is again an adjective describing what kind of sinners they are, *"ungodly sinners."* And what deeds have caused them to be ungodly sinners? It was because of the *"hard speeches"* they spoke against God. Hard speeches would be blasphemous and irreverent against God, His truths, His ways, and His people. And whether it was against His people or Him, it all comes down to being done against God. It is against them because they came against Him.

My friend, there is a real judgment coming to these people. They will face a real hell. Once again, it would do as Jude would say, **ALL** of us to take this warning to heart. Next time we want to look at porn, have road rage toward another or something as simple as gossip, or not forgive our brothers and sisters in Christ, we need to reflect on how much God is against a sinful lifestyle.

1st Peter 4:17 states, *"For the time is come that judgment must begin at the house of God: and if it first begin at us, what shall the end be of them that obey not the gospel of God?"* Although a Christian won't face hell, we will still be judged on what we have done and might have to suffer in the flesh because of some of those deeds. These warnings should help the believer to strive to live and walk in the power God has given us over sin.

Chapter 10

Deplorables

"These are murmurers, complainers, walking after their own lusts; and their mouth speaketh great swelling words, having men's persons in admiration because of advantage. But, beloved, remember ye the words which were spoken before of the apostles of our Lord Jesus Christ; How that they told you there should be mockers in the last time, who should walk after their own ungodly lusts. These be they who separate themselves, sensual, having not the Spirit."
Jude verses 16-19.

Again, Jude wants them to understand how to identify these false prophets, how they act, and their true intentions; *"These are murmurers, complainers...."* These people had no or had lost all faith in God's abilities and were finding fault with God's plans for their lives.

As we mentioned at the beginning of the book, the church at the time of Jude's writing was going through many trials and persecution. It is easy to serve God when everything is going well in our lives, but when times start getting hard, we can find ourselves having trouble trusting in God and begin to murmur about our situation.

I had this happen in my life just this past week before I started studying these Scriptures. Life had been going so great; there was no drama in the house, all of our bills were paid, and God was opening doors for me to minister; it felt like I had the world by the tail. But as most of you can probably empathize, how quickly a day can make a change.

It all started when I was sitting at home waiting for my wife to get back from dropping off the grandkids with their mother. My wife watches them while their mother is at work. I got a phone call from her that said, *"meet me at the parts place. The car is acting up."*

I met her at the parts place and had them run a diagnostic on the car to see what was going on. The parts man told me that one of the cylinders was misfiring. He said it could be a sensor, an ignition coil, or a spark plug.

That didn't bother me much as I have changed all of those things before with relative ease. I asked the parts man how much the ignition coil was, and he said one hundred dollars. **ONE HUNDRED DOLLARS!** I was shocked because I normally paid around $54 for this part, but unfortunately, that part had doubled because of the failing economy.

Well, anyone that knows me knows I will not pay a lot of money for anything, so I told my wife she could drive my car while we waited on a part to come the next day from online. I had an old work van, so I drove it while we waited. I knew the part would be in the next day around 3 pm, so I wasn't all that concerned.

While waiting on the part to arrive, I decided to get the valve cover gasket off and remove the old ignition coil so the job would be quick and easy when the part came in. **BUT,** when I was taking the wiring plug off the ignition coil, the wires came apart from the plug!!! This would mean ordering that part and waiting another day for it to come in since the parts place doesn't sell it; it can only be gotten at the dealer, and I knew I wasn't going to pay what a dealer would charge.

Sure enough, the part came on time, so I told my wife she would probably be able to use her car to drop the kids off. I told her, *"This won't take me but about 5 minutes to install."*

I rushed out to do the work, and just as I said, I had it on in only 5 minutes. Filled with joy and excitement, knowing life was about to return to the way it was, I started the car only to discover that it was still running poorly. I figured it was the spark plug, so I ran to the parts place to pick one up and began to remove the plug.

WELL, while removing the spark plug, the old spark plug broke off in the engine. Anyone that knows about engines knows that is NOT a good thing and can cost A LOT of money to repair. I prayed, *"Please, God, help me get this out!"* And that He did! I was back in business!!!

I told my wife she would need to drive my car another day or two while I get a mechanic to put the other plugs in. After the first one broke off, I was too afraid to attempt the others. Looking back on it now, that was dumb. The mechanic could have broken one as I did and would have had to charge to fix the head just as much as if I had broken it off. The bottom line is that the mechanic charged $200 just to put in three plugs, which took all of 5 minutes is my guess.

I went to pick the car up and pay the mechanic. My wife was with me, and while going to pick up her car, I smiled and said, *"Looks like you will finally be able to drive your car tomorrow, and I can get mine back!"* I went in to pay the mechanic and asked him, *"Did you get all the plugs in, okay?"* He said, *"Yes, but you have another problem."* REALLY! Come on, give me a break, I thought to myself!

I asked him what the problem was now. He informed me that the radiator was leaking very badly and I wouldn't be able to drive it far. I told him I would take care of that, dropped her car off at the house, and headed for the parts place again.

When I got to the parts place and inquired if they had the radiator, they said yes. Once again, I had high hopes this journey was about over. That is, until I found out how much the part would be. THREE HUNDRED AND FIFTY DOLLARS!!! To me, that was highway robbery. I told him to forget it and went home to order online again, which cost only one hundred and thirty dollars, but I would have to wait a week to get it.

While waiting on the radiator, my wife called again coming home with the grandkids, and said, *"Your car is acting up."* I thought, what are we going to do now? With two cars down, we would all have to share the work van, and it only had two seats. My wife would never ride in it because of everything in the van. So, I had her drive to the parts place. We checked it out only to find that it also needed an ignition coil. Luckily when I ordered the one for her car, I was able to buy four for under the price of one, so I was able to go ahead and fix that right away.

123

Well, a long week of me waiting and having to drive my old work van finally came to an end. I removed her old radiator, put the new one in, and changed the oil. I also bought some brighter lights to put in her car since hers were the old type and very dim.

Confident again that all was well, the following day, bright and early, I headed for the grocery store and Walmart to get some things before she would be back with the grandchild. While heading home, I get a call from her again, which isn't normal. When I answered, she asked how far I was from the house, and I told her I was about 20 minutes away, so she said she was going to get her daughter to drop the grandchild off because the car wouldn't start.

Then she asked, *"Did you put the battery in correctly?"* I could feel my pressure mounting as I said back, *"OF COURSE I PUT THE BATTERY BACK CORRECTLY! I THINK I KNOW HOW TO PUT A BATTERY IN!!!"*

I get home to find the car battery dead as a nail. I knew it had finally gone out, and there was no need to charge it. It was old and ready to go out, but I thought, couldn't it have lasted at least another month so I could get a breath? But knowing that this really shouldn't take long either, I hopped in the car and headed to Home Depot to get the battery. Why there? Because they are normally cheaper than anyone else on car batteries.

With my fingers crossed, after putting the new battery in, I cranked the car, and YES! IT STARTED AND WAS RUNNING GREAT!!! Finally, all my days of struggles were over. I could get back to relaxation and, just as important, get my car back. I decided that I needed to test drive it before handing it over to my wife.

The first mile, everything was fantastic. I smiled, turned on the radio, and was singing along when all of a sudden, the speedometer dropped to zero, my RPM gauge started moving rapidly up and down, the ABS light came on, and the transmission started acting up. I couldn't believe it!!!

Disappointed, I drove back home and looked online to try and diagnose the problem. I discovered that it would be my modular, so I looked it up online. The price... **$900 REBUILT!!!** Thank God I could replace it myself and save on the installation cost!

I decided to call some of the salvage yards before buying it and was able to purchase a used one for $125. I got it, installed it on the car, and **VOILA**! It was running and acting like new. Thank God!!!

The following day I had to go to Walmart early again. You can tell I spend a lot of time there. I jumped in my car, turned the key, and NOTHING!!! The car didn't even make a sound. No clicking, NOTHING!!!

Because I knew she would need her car before I got back, I just got in the old, trustworthy work van and headed to Walmart. While driving there, I told the Lord, *"We have to talk!"* I began to let the Lord know that I wasn't saying He hadn't blessed us abundantly because He has, but I was having a problem with all that was going on. I reminded Him, as if He didn't know, that I not only tithe but give far above the tithe. I told Him how faithful we are to church, considering the distance we travel to get there. I went on talking about how I try to read the Bible, pray, and live a good life, blah, blah, blah. I heard nothing from the Spirit during or immediately after I had run my rant.

I went into the store frustrated, gathered my stuff, and started back home. While driving home, I heard the Spirit as if He said, *"Are you finished with your rant now?"* I said to myself, yes. I then felt Him saying something like this, paraphrasing, of course. *"When you get home, get the key to YOUR car from your wife, and your car will start."* I could almost hear Him add, "idiot."

What happened was I had her key, which only would start her car, and my key worked on either car. I felt like a fool after spewing all my frustrations out on God, only to find out, He had nothing to do with it; it was all my fault. Have you ever had anything similar in your life where you finally lost it and began to lash out against God? If not, I thank God for your incredible holiness in the life you live. I've not made it there yet.

After it all settled down, the Holy Spirit gently reminded me how I should have acted differently. He reminded me that I should be grateful for all God has done for my family and me. I have a home paid for, a nice bed to sleep in with sheets and comfortable pillows. I have heat and air, food in the cabinets and refrigerator, and clothes on my back and in my closet. I have money in the bank that helped pay for all the parts, a Christian wife, and a family that prays for me. I have not only one car but three, so I never had to be without a car during the whole experience, and all of those are paid for. I have a great church with an awesome pastor and staff. I have a lot of church members that love us. I live in America, where I am not only free to go to church but free to have my own personal Bible, not one but many. My wife and I have pretty good health at our age. He reminded me that most car payments are over $500 a month, and I have had three cars for over five years, and with all that has gone wrong with them, it would have only come to about six payments on one car. But the most precious thing that I should have been thankful for is the salvation that Jesus Christ purchased for me so that I wouldn't have to suffer eternally in hell.

The Holy Spirit had a way of getting me back to reality. I had no reason to complain, and I had let a little bit of inconvenience take my joy and contentment away. In America, we all are so blessed that we should never complain. If you feel the need to, just get a copy of the "Foxe's Book of Martyrs," and you will soon see just how trivial your problems are compared to theirs.

The people Jude was referring to were murmuring like the children of Israel when God had taken them out of Egypt. His plan was to give them a land flowing with milk and honey. But, because life had gotten hard, they could not care less about what God had already done nor where He was going to bring them. They were hungry; God fed them. They were thirsty, and God would give them water. They would confront armies; although they were not warriors, God would deliver them. They fussed about every trial they faced in life, not knowing that some of these were to make them strong people.

God finally had enough and didn't allow them the blessing He wanted them to have. God only does what is best for His people. When we don't trust Him and fuss about our situation, it shows Him that we don't trust Him with our lives. If we can't trust Him with our lives, how can we trust that we will make it to Heaven?

Not only did they fuss about their situation, they then began comparing their lives with those around them. They went as far as to say life was better as a slave in Egypt than to die in the wilderness. They didn't do this once; they did it many times, even after seeing God provide for every situation. The Bible says, *"For we dare not make ourselves of the number, or compare ourselves with some that commend themselves: but they measuring themselves by themselves, and comparing themselves among themselves, are not wise."* 2nd Corinthians 10:12.

They looked at how easily worldly people had it while they were suffering for Christ. They looked at the surface and had no idea what these people's lives were. We look at rich or famous people and think what a wonderful life they must have. But in reality, we don't see the pain, anguish, loneliness, and more they face daily; and many times without Christ to help. We fail to remember Mark 8:36, which says, *"For what shall it profit a man, if he shall gain the whole world, and lose his own soul?"* We look at the temporal, forgetting, *"Whereas ye know not what shall be on the morrow. For what is your life? It is even a vapour, that appeareth for a little time, and then vanisheth away."* James 4:14.

We, as Christians, are not here to live an abundant life as far as material things go, no matter what the television preacher is saying. We are here to be witnesses for Christ. We have been called to suffer with Him, and if we suffer with Him, according to the Bible, we will also reign with Him. Our abundant life comes from the peace, joy, and love that Christ provides us through the Holy Spirit, things that the world cannot give.

Job was a perfect example of how we should respond to God when going through trials. His wife didn't understand why God would allow her husband to suffer after being a faithful servant to God. She wanted Job to compromise and just die. But Job said she spoke like a foolish woman. Job knew that life comes with good and bad, but God will always be faithful to His promises and children. And as we have read, God was.

My Christian brothers and sisters, we, in America, have been spoiled, but we are about to see the church go through things we have never seen before. We better keep our faith through Bible reading, prayer, and fasting, *"Looking unto Jesus the author and finisher of our faith; who for the joy that was set before him endured the cross, despising the shame, and is set down at the right hand of the throne of God."* Hebrews 12:2. As long as we keep our eyes on Him, we won't be able to see the things around us that can cause us to lose hope and stray.

Next, Jude described them as *"walking after their own lusts."* When you look at this statement in the original Greek, we find that it was their desires leading them, not them going after their desires. To give you an example,

129

Satan will first tempt you with a sinful action, such as pornography. At first, you feel the Holy Spirit warning you not to go to the site where the pornography is. But you, like King David, decide to look instead of turning away.

At first, you feel guilty and maybe even dirty, and you should if you are a born-again believer. But, if you continue to resist the Holy Spirit and give yourself unto that fleshly desire, it won't be long before the desire has complete control over you. You don't have the power anymore to turn away, and it has you under its grip and power. You willfully submit to its guidance.

This is the result for these people. They might have been good workers in the church. They might have had a decent life, but because they turned to their desires, their desires now have control. They are no longer suitable for the church or themselves. They destroy not only their lives but anyone that is near them. We need to remember, unlike God, who has our best in mind, Satan comes *"...to steal, and to kill, and to destroy...."* The little pleasure he offers is only to bind you to his will, and he will take away all that is dear to you.

Besides the sin now controlling these people's lives, they have become masterful with their tongues to convince people they are right in their beliefs and practices. See what Jude said about them, *"and their mouth speaketh great swelling words, having men's persons in admiration because of advantage."*

They would use flattery as a way to get what they wanted. Most of the time, we see this with people trying to get ahead in the world. They may flatter the boss and complement them to be noticed and liked hoping one day the boss will put them in a high position with higher pay. People in places like the movie industry want to hang around the person that has made the top big movies, hoping that by their being around them, others may take notice of them or expect the person at the top will use them in their next new blockbuster.

I am so glad that God is not a respecter of persons. It does no good to try and flatter God; He knows the true intents of your heart. He doesn't care about your social or financial standing; we are all equal in His sight. No one can get to Heaven by what one can bring to the table or who they know besides the Lord Jesus Christ. God can not be bribed or intimidated. He is all in all and needs no one to advance Him.

Jude then has a message to the church members that are near to his heart, *"But, beloved, remember ye the words which were spoken before of the apostles of our Lord Jesus Christ." Jude verse 17.* Here he is telling them not just to remember but be reminded or mindful of the words spoken, and he wants the spoken words to be continually at the forefront of their minds.

What better instruction could Jude give them than bury themselves in the Word? Jude refers to the words that Christ spoke to them and His apostles. Because the apostles knew what Christ said, they, too, were sharing the words of Christ. They showed plainly that they were speaking God's Word and not their own, *"For this cause also thank we God without ceasing, because, when ye received the word of God which ye heard of us, ye received it not as the word of men, but as it is in truth, the word of God, which effectually worketh also in you that believe."* 1st Thessalonians 2:13. It is this Word that they can trust in and stand firm.

We find in John 1:1 just who the Word is, *"In the beginning was the Word, and the Word was with God, and the Word was God."* And in John 1:14, *"And the Word was made flesh, and dwelt among us, (and we beheld his glory, the glory as of the only begotten of the Father,) full of grace and truth."* Jesus Christ, Himself is the Word of God. He was here in the beginning, and he helped fashion all we see. Nothing is hidden from Him, and there is nothing He doesn't know. Let's look at a few verses to show how important the Word of God is and why Jude said to keep it in our minds.

The Word is the spiritual bread we need for our spirit man to survive, *"...man doth not live by bread only, but by every word that proceedeth out of the mouth of the LORD doth man live."* Deuteronomy 8:3

The apostles knew that they would only be able to make it in this life through Christ, the living Word, *"Then Simon Peter answered him, Lord, to whom shall we go? thou hast the words of eternal life."* John 6:68. Only by trusting in Christ and His Word can we live not only in this flesh but also eternally in Heaven.

One of my favorite verses says, *"Thy word have I hid in mine heart, that I might not sin against thee."* Psalms 119:11. It is through the Word of God that you can overcome sin. And according to Psalm 119:105, we can have the Word keep us on the right path on our journey, *"Thy word is a lamp unto my feet, and a light unto my path."*

The Word of God can teach us the way we should go and help teach others, *"All scripture is given by inspiration of God, and is profitable for doctrine, for reproof, for correction, for instruction in righteousness:"* 2nd Timothy 3:16.

Through the Word, you grow in faith: *"So then faith cometh by hearing, and hearing by the word of God."* Romans 10:17. The Word is part of our weapons to fight against the enemy, *"And take the helmet of salvation, and the sword of the Spirit, which is the word of God..."* Ephesians 6:17.

Now can you see why Jude admonished them to keep the Word of God in their minds? The Word of God will keep you pure, true, faithful, obedient, separated from the world, and fill you with wisdom and knowledge. It can also identify what you may be lacking in your life as well as why you do what you do, *"For the word of God is quick, and powerful, and sharper than any two-edged sword, piercing even to the dividing asunder of soul and spirit, and of the joints and marrow, and is a discerner of the thoughts and intents of the heart."* Hebrews 4:12. You can trust the Word of God for EVERYTHING you need in your life!!!

Jude told them that Christ and His servants warned, *"...there should be mockers in the last time, who should walk after their own ungodly lusts."* Jude verse 18. It should not have come as a surprise to the church in Jude's day. God doesn't want to send judgment; therefore, He warns us what to watch for and does it before judgment comes.

No one, not the people of that day, nor us, once we have heard the Word of God, can blame God for judgment that He might send because His Word warns us what will bring it on. His Word not only warns us what not to do but shows us how to make it through. We need to look to God's Word on how to survive, not to what man is trying to tell us.

Think of all the warnings God had sent in the past before He brought judgment. In the beginning, God warned Adam and Eve not to take the fruit of the tree of *"knowledge of good and evil,"* or they would die. Yet they didn't heed His warning, and everyone now under Adam is physically under the curse of death. You are under the spiritual curse if you don't accept the blood of Christ as your atonement for Adam's disobedience against God, because the curse has been passed down through Adam's bloodline.

God warned the people of Noah's day that if they didn't repent, He would send a flood and kill them. Yet they didn't listen. He warned even an evil Pharaoh idol worshipper if He didn't let His people go, He would send judgment, yet he didn't listen. He warned the children of Israel not to murmur or complain, or they wouldn't enter into the land flowing with milk and honey. He warned Balaam through a talking donkey not to come against the children of Israel, yet he didn't listen. God even warned Herod through a dream his wife had not to come against Christ. Yet he didn't listen.

We could go on and on about how God always warned before He sent judgment. Most of the time, God sends warnings either from Himself or through His servants first; but He will ALWAYS send the warning.

134

Amos 3:7 says, *"Surely the Lord GOD will do nothing, but he revealeth his secret unto his servants the prophets."* God is still sending warnings out to people today. He has warned in His Word that if we reject Christ, we will die and go to hell. He has warned in His Word that if we live a disobedient life, He will bring judgment, and we will suffer. He has warned that the end is near, and if we don't repent and come to Christ, we will face the Great Tribulation, which will cause such suffering as never seen before by man and end in destruction.

These *"mockers"* that Jude talked about were people who approached God not in a serious manner. The word *"mockers"* could also be interpreted as false teachers. They had no fear of His judgment of their lifestyle. And they were teaching others that God, in essence, was a God of love and wouldn't punish you for the life you live. Once again, we see that their desire was what was leading their lives, not God, not themselves, but their passions and desires. You could say that they were led by Satan, the one whom they were serving at the time.

The Bible tells us that we can't serve two masters. Matthew 6:24 states, *"No man can serve two masters: for either he will hate the one, and love the other; or else he will hold to the one, and despise the other. Ye cannot serve God and mammon."* Paul in Romans 6:16 future explains, *"Know ye not, that to whom ye yield yourselves servants to obey, his servants ye are to whom ye obey; whether of sin unto death, or of obedience unto righteousness?"* You can not straddle the fence. You must make up your mind to follow Christ fully or to fulfill the lust of your flesh and suffer the judgment from that. God is a jealous God. When we serve the will of ourselves, we, in essence, have made Satan our God. In the Ten Commandments, God stated that you could not serve any God but Him. He will not be shared. With Him, it's all or nothing.

Jude describes, *"These be they who separate themselves."* They are unstable and have no foundation. The Bible says, *"And if a house be divided against itself, that house cannot stand."* Mark 3:25. Satan is always causing division, and he primarily attacks the church. He knows that if he can get people in the church to fuss, bicker, and gossip, it won't be long before the church will split and possibly fall. I have seen this happen with something as minor as what color to paint the church.

The people that Jude is referring to are causing division in the body of Christ. They are separating themselves from other Christians, from the truth, and from giving their time in the church ministry. They want to live out their beliefs no matter what Christ's Word says. They feel that they have more wisdom than anyone else in the church. They refuse to be instructed. Furthermore, they don't want to participate in anything requiring their time or money. Church, for them, is about getting everything they need and then leaving without benefiting anyone else.

It boggles my mind that these people could have thought this way, considering all the Scriptures that are entirely opposite of what they were teaching and doing. Take, for instance, separating themselves from the church. The Word of God explicitly tells us in Hebrews 10:25, *"Not forsaking the assembling of ourselves together, as the manner of some is; but exhorting one another: and so much the more, as ye see the day approaching.*" In Romans chapter 12, Paul gives a whole list of how Christians should act. In verse one, He instructs us to be a living sacrifice to God. In verse two, we are not to be conformed to this world but think differently than the word does. Verse three teaches us that we are not to think of ourselves more highly than others. Verses four through eight let us know that we are all one body working together with God's gifts. In verse nine, Paul tells us to hate evil, and in verse ten, to love each other with a pure love and not show partiality. In verse eleven, it shows we should not only work but work hard to serve the Lord. Verse thirteen shows we should care for people in the church who have needs. Verse sixteen says that we should not be wise in our own conceits. These scriptures alone should dispel everything these false teachers claimed. And yet, today, there are people in the church acting the same way these false teachers did.

If a person is truly in Christ Jesus, they should reflect what Christ is all about, which is love. Love for one another and love for God. It was because of that great love for others that God sent His Son, and His Son willingly gave up His life for rotten sinners that couldn't give anything back.

We find God always reaching to man. His attributes are merciful, gracious, slow to anger, abounding in steadfast love and faithfulness, forgiving, and not willing that any should perish but all come to repentance. He is quick to hear the cry of His people and to run to their aid. He is our protector, our guide, and our loving Father. He has promised He will never leave or forsake us, that He will stick by us closer than a brother.

Do you have these qualities? If not, which ones are lacking in your life? We all should strive to have all of these abiding within us so we can be a blessing to not only God but each other.

Then Jude says they were *"sensual."* Sensual means the natural man. So they are worldly-minded instead of Godly-minded. They spend more time doing what they want than spending time with God. If they don't see, hear, touch, or feel it, they won't believe it. Their physical senses guide them. They are just like the wild animals in the fields and have no conscience or morality.

Their *"having not the Spirit"* was why these false teachers were the way they were. They knew no better. The Bible describes a person that doesn't have the Holy Spirit living inside them as a dead man. I have gone to many funerals and have never seen a dead person react to anything around them. I have sung at several funerals, and not once has the deceased person told me that I did an awful job. For that matter, they never said I did good either, thank God, or I might not be here today!

You can yell at them, hit them, spit at them, or do anything else you please, and they won't respond. NOTHING moves them, and you can't teach them ANYTHING. Their hearts are cold and indifferent, and they care less about those around them. Everything about them starts to decay, and they begin to smell after a while. No wonder the Bible uses the analogy of a dead person describing the lost.

Since Jude mentioned they didn't have the Spirit, it would do us good to see the difference the Spirit makes in a person. Notice first, the spirit Jude spoke of was with a capital "S," which means the Holy Spirit. John 16:13 lets us know that the Spirit will give us the truth, *"Howbeit when he, the Spirit of truth, is come, he will guide you into all truth: for he shall not speak of himself; but whatsoever he shall hear, that shall he speak: and he will shew you things to come."*

We know in Romans 8:2 that the Spirit frees us from the law of sin and death, *"For the law of the Spirit of life in Christ Jesus hath made me free from the law of sin and death."* We know if you don't have the Spirit as these false prophets, you are not a part of Christ, *"But ye are not in the flesh, but in the Spirit, if so be that the Spirit of God dwell in you. Now if any man have not the Spirit of Christ, he is none of his."* Romans 8:9.

Romans 8:26 lets us know it is the Spirit within us that makes intercession when we don't know what to pray, *"Likewise the Spirit also helpeth our infirmities: for we know not what we should pray for as we ought: but the Spirit itself maketh intercession for us with groanings which cannot be uttered."*

According to 1st Corinthians 6:11, we are sanctified by the Spirit, *"And such were some of you: but ye are washed, but ye are sanctified, but ye are justified in the name of the Lord Jesus, and by the Spirit of our God."* It is the Spirit that gives each believer his gifts to minister. Galatians 5:16 lets us know that if we walk in the Spirit, we won't fulfill the lust of the flesh.

Galatians in 5:22-23 shows us what should be manifested in our lives, *"But the fruit of the Spirit is love, joy, peace, longsuffering, gentleness, goodness, faith, Meekness, temperance: against such there is no law."* Ephesians 6:17 calls the Spirit the Word of God, *"And take the helmet of salvation, and the sword of the Spirit, which is the word of God..."* I'd say that having the Holy Spirit inside is a prerequisite of being saved, don't you?

These false teachers probably truly believed they were saved. It would do us all good to do as 2nd Corinthians 13:5 says, *"Examine yourselves, whether ye be in the faith; prove your own selves. Know ye not your own selves, how that Jesus Christ is in you, except ye be reprobates?"*

Chapter 11

A Different Breed

"But ye, beloved, building up yourselves on your most holy faith, praying in the Holy Ghost, Keep yourselves in the love of God, looking for the mercy of our Lord Jesus Christ unto eternal life. And of some have compassion, making a difference: And others save with fear, pulling them out of the fire; hating even the garment spotted by the flesh. Now unto him that is able to keep you from falling, and to present you faultless before the presence of his glory with exceeding joy, To the only wise God our Saviour, be glory and majesty, dominion and power, both now and ever. Amen."
Jude verses 20-25.

"But ye, beloved." Jude now turns his focus on the true believers of the church and how they are to respond to everything he has warned them about. In these next few verses, Jude gives them examples of what to do to stay strong.

The first thing Jude mentions is an action verb, *"building up yourselves."* Building here means it is something that we should be doing daily. Just coming to Christ and being born-again is not all we need to do; we should start at that point and add to it.

When it says *"up yourselves,"* it can also mean not just you but your brothers and sisters in Christ Jesus. Notice it says *"building up,"* not tearing down. Far too often, I see members of the body of Christ putting down others. They judge others in their ministry, making statements that put that individual down or as if they are not doing their job correctly. Unless God has given you that position, it is not in your job description to judge another's proficiency on how they are performing the job God put them in. They seem to attack the pastor or a Sunday School teacher especially.

It is all I can do not to say, "and how faithful are YOU to the church? How much have YOU done for the Lord? How much of your time do YOU give to serving and studying God's Word? How much do YOU give in the offering to support the church and its ministries?"

Most of the time, the answer would be very little. They don't mind laying out to watch a ball game or spending the day playing golf, or going fishing instead of going to church. People need to be careful in judging others because the Bible tells us that if we judge others, we will be judged in the same manner. In other words, if you judge them on how they are doing their job for Christ, God will judge you on how well you did your part. Now that I got that out of my system, let's move on.

As a former home remodeling contractor, the first thing you MUST do before building onto anything is to make sure the foundation you are building on is firm. The example of which person's foundation you build upon and the result of that decision is found in Matthew 7:24-27, *"Therefore whosoever heareth these sayings of mine, and doeth them, I will liken him unto a wise man, which built his house upon a rock: And the rain descended, and the floods came, and the winds blew, and beat upon that house; and it fell not: for it was founded upon a rock. And every one that heareth these sayings of mine, and doeth them not, shall be likened unto a foolish man, which built his house upon the sand: And the rain descended, and the floods came, and the winds blew, and beat upon that house; and it fell: and great was the fall of it.* " Without a firm foundation, your house WILL SURLY FALL!

And what is that firm foundation? 1st Corinthians 3:10-11, *" According to the grace of God which is given unto me, as a wise masterbuilder, I have laid the foundation, and another buildeth thereon. But let every man take heed how he buildeth thereupon. For other foundation can no man lay than that is laid, which is Jesus Christ.* " It is none other than Christ, the stone the world rejected, the Chief Cornerstone. He is the firm foundation, the solid foundation, the everlasting foundation, the tested foundation; He is the only foundation to trust!

Just what should we be building on top of the foundation and helping others build as well? It is *"your most holy faith.* " This faith is the Gospel of our Lord Jesus Christ and the writing of his apostles that revealed what He said. It is building one another and ourselves in the knowledge and holiness of our faith. This is not faith in man but *"most holy faith.* " It is most holy, which leads men to repentance and to hate sin. It causes us to love and obey God and live a righteous life which is the opposite of the false teachers Jude had just written about.

Everyone that accepts the Lord Jesus Christ is given a measure of faith. That has been provided by God. But, we

143

should not be satisfied with just what was given; we need to build on that faith according to this Scripture. The measure of faith that was given will take you to heaven; the faith you build upon that will take you through life's troubles.

2nd Peter is a sister book to Jude. Verses 5-7 of chapter 1 tell some of the things we should be building on the foundation of Christ. And at the start, he tells us to do this right away, as if time depended upon it.

The first is moral excellence or virtue. Isn't it amazing that Peter felt that being morally right should be the first thing to build on? All through the Scriptures, you see where immorality destroyed people's lives and walk with God. It was immorality that helped cause the children of Israel to be judged, and it was immorality that caused trouble in the life of Samson and King David.

I have seen many pastors lose their church and testimony because they yielded to lust in a moment of weakness. One moment of pleasure can destroy a lifetime of ministry. That is why they said Billy Graham always had someone with him. He knew the dangers of being alone with the opposite sex.

Virtue and integrity come together. Integrity is what you do when no one is watching. Earlier in this book, I told of how Satan uses sex and immorality as a portal to enter into a man's spirit. By man, I mean mankind because it affects both men and women. The man mainly falls from the lust of the eyes, and women tend to fall because of the mental aspect of sex and love. Those so-called romance books are mostly

144

filled with vivid imaginary scenes placed in the mind. Our imagination causes us to stray from God often. That is why we are warned to renew our mind and keep it pure in thought.

Paul in Philippians 4:8 gives us a guideline of what our minds should be focused on, *"Finally, brethren, whatsoever things are true, whatsoever things are honest, whatsoever things are just, whatsoever things are pure, whatsoever things are lovely, whatsoever things are of good report; if there be any virtue, and if there be any praise, think on these things."*

The next thing Peter says to add is *"knowledge."* This is not the type of knowledge that these false prophets had. They trusted in man's wisdom which can lead you astray. This knowledge Jude is talking about can not be obtained at man's institutes of learning. God's Word tells us, *"My people are destroyed for lack of knowledge: because thou hast rejected knowledge, I will also reject thee, that thou shalt be no priest to me: seeing thou hast forgotten the law of thy God, I will also forget thy children."* Hosea 4:6. Proverbs 9:10 tells us where to begin in adding knowledge, *"The fear of the Lord is the beginning of wisdom: and the knowledge of the holy is understanding."*

James 1:5 tells how we can obtain some of that knowledge, *"If any of you lack wisdom, let him ask of God, that giveth to all men liberally, and upbraideth not; and it shall be given him."* Proverbs 2:6 tells where this knowledge comes from, *"For the Lord giveth wisdom: out of his mouth cometh knowledge and understanding."*

God wants us to know His Word, His Law, and what He wants and expects from us. The knowledge of God is so vital that He places it above our works, *"And Samuel said, Hath the Lord as great delight in burnt offerings and sacrifices, as in obeying the voice of the Lord? Behold, to obey is better than sacrifice, and to hearken than the fat of rams."* 1st Samuel 15:22. He is not saying that God doesn't want our offerings and works, but He wants us to know His ways and truth, so when we give and serve, we do it in a manner that will be pleasing to Him.

The next thing to put on the foundation is "temperance," or self-control. You must first have the knowledge of God and what He expects before you can add temperance. Of course, the evil inclinations and appetites that our flesh desires are meant to be kept under control. 2nd Corinthians 10:5 says, *"Casting down imaginations, and every high thing that exalteth itself against the knowledge of God, and bringing into captivity every thought to the obedience of Christ…"* Satan is like what the old timers used to say, *"If you give him an inch, he will take a mile."*

Self-control is a battle that we must face almost every minute of everyday. Paul said, *"I find then a law, that, when I would do good, evil is present with me. For I delight in the law of God after the inward man: But I see another law in my members, warring against the law of my mind, and bringing me into captivity to the law of sin which is in my members. O wretched man that I am! who shall deliver me from the body of this death?"* Romans 7:21-24. We all have that battle within us that are believers in Christ. Therefore we are to *"Mortify therefore your members which are upon the*

146

earth; fornication, uncleanness, inordinate affection, evil concupiscence, and covetousness, which is idolatry; For which things' sake the wrath of God cometh on the children of disobedience: In the which ye also walked some time, when ye lived in them. But now ye also put off all these; anger, wrath, malice, blasphemy, filthy communication out of your mouth." Colossians 3:5-8. We can only do this if we keep ourselves in God's Word and obey His commands. It takes the strength of the Holy Spirit for us to be overcomers.

Then comes the one that I am sure almost every believer has been warned not to pray for, *"patience."* And why do people warn others not to pray for that? The answer is found in Romans 5:3, *"And not only so, but we glory in tribulations also: knowing that tribulation worketh patience."* But without tribulations, you don't get what Paul said next, which is experience and, with experience, hope.

What is Paul trying to say? Without us going through hard times in our lives, we can never learn that we can put our complete confidence in the power and might of our Lord Jesus Christ. The battles and darkness we go through make the light shine so much brighter when we get through it. How can I witness to a person who is facing a problem that is beyond human help if I have never had the experience of seeing God work a miracle in my own life? I know God can supply my needs because He has in the past. I know God can triumph over my enemies because He has done so in the past. I know God can heal my broken heart because He has done so in the past. I know God can heal my body because He has healed it in the past. He is not only omnipresent, meaning He can be everywhere at the same time. He is not only omniscient, which means He knows all, but thank God He is also omnipotent, meaning He has power over ALL. As the old song says, *"Our trials only come to make us strong."*

Once again, you wouldn't be able to have patience had you not put all the other things mentioned above in place. And certainly, you wouldn't be able to add the next thing had you not put all the other things in your life, which is *"godliness."* Godliness could be interpreted as holiness or as *"character."*

Character is what people see in the way you live your life. They can see you are different in the way you walk and talk versus how the world walks and talks. It is one thing to say you are a Christian and another to have walked in obedience and been faithful to Christ. When you have walked so close to Christ, the fragrance of His holiness radiates through you. It comes from sticking by Him when you wanted to quit but didn't.

It reminds me of a prayer I heard a man give. He said, *"God, make me a sponge so that when temptations and trials begin to squeeze in my life, from me, they will see your glory running out of my being."* This type of godliness was shown in Christ; because of that, we can now enjoy having it by Christ Jesus. 1st Timothy 3:16, *"And without controversy great is the mystery of godliness: God was manifest in the flesh, justified in the Spirit, seen of angels, preached unto the Gentiles, believed on in the world, received up into glory."* Through Christ, we will not only be able to reflect His glory but, one day, be risen with Him in the air to live forever.

Character is not something you can purchase; it is something you have worked for. If you have ever been in the military, the drill sergeants are masters in building character. How do they do this? They make you submit to authority, put you through strenuous tests on your body and mind, make you watch out for your partner, and teach you no man is an island by himself. It is those things that build character. Once fully being obedient to following the Holy Spirit, it will build your spiritual character that others can see.

By placing all the former building blocks in place, we can move on to *"brotherly kindness."* This is when we get to the place where we care about others and are not just focusing on ourselves and our needs. Selfishness is an attribute of the flesh. You don't have to learn it; it is embedded in human nature. The world even tells us that we better watch out for number one because no one else will. But that shouldn't be an attribute of a saint of God.

If you see a person in the church who is easy to get angry or upset when they don't get their way, you can almost rest assured they have not been placing these building blocks in their lives. Also, when you see people who are jealous over another's ability to preach, teach, or sing, they obviously don't have brother love as they ought.

When you have brotherly love, you should feel proud of that person and be willing to take a back seat. I love my kids, so I want them to achieve more in life than I thought possible for myself. I swell with pride when I see them doing that. If you want to know if you have developed in your walk with God, just take a moment and evaluate how you react toward your brother and sister in Christ.

149

Peter's last instruction on building on the foundation is *"charity."* The word charity in the original is *"agape."* This is known as a Godly love, a pure love, a love that goes beyond anything that comes against it. Once you have the agape love inside of you, you can not only love your brother and sisters in Christ, but you can even love your enemies. You will begin to change the way you look at lost sinners. Instead of looking with disgust when you see a drunkard passed out on the street or a prostitute walking down the boulevard, you will feel compassion and godly sorrow for that individual. This is the type of love every born-again believer needs to strive for.

1ˢᵗ Corinthians 13:4-7 gives a picture of how agape love acts, *"Charity suffereth long, and is kind; charity envieth not; charity vaunteth not itself, is not puffed up, Doth not behave itself unseemly, seeketh not her own, is not easily provoked, thinketh no evil; Rejoiceth not in iniquity, but rejoiceth in the truth; Beareth all things, believeth all things, hopeth all things, endureth all things."*

If you don't do these things above, you are not as holy as you might think. I have seen people that talk a good game; they act like they are godly in every aspect of their lives. However, it is not long till the heart is revealed. Whenever I think of this behavior, my mind goes back to a singer in a group I know. When you talk to that individual, they talk the godly talk, they always seem to have a smile on their face, and they seem to have a gentle spirit. But I have seen the other side of that person as well. They are very judgmental of others and even blast things that lost people do instead to witnessing to them about God's love and showing compassion.

150

When a person acts like that, they are NOT holy; they are SELF-RIGHTEOUS. I have a hard time being around those people, and Christ did too. They are the modern-day version of the Pharisees in Jesus' day. They speak swelling words, but their actions prove they don't have a love of God in them as they should. Paraphrasing what Jesus said, before you go around correcting everyone else on their behavior, take a look deep within your own life. I am sure if you ask the Holy Spirit to reveal your problems, He will; when He does, you will soon find out you have too much to work on yourself to try to work on others.

Jude then instructs us to be *"praying in the Holy Ghost."* This verse has been debated for a long time on what praying in the Holy Ghost means. Some believe the only way to pray in the Holy Ghost is with some divine language that God imparts to you.

They derive this from the book of Acts, which talks about the Holy Spirit coming to reveal Himself to the saints after Christ ascended to heaven. It says in Acts 2:4, *"And they were all filled with the Holy Ghost, and began to speak with other tongues, as the Spirit gave them utterance."* That verse is where there is a deep division in certain denominations as to precisely what that meant. To the people who believe that praying in the Holy Ghost is speaking in that Divine language, then that would mean that not everyone will be able to do what Jude just had instructed to do because not everyone has the gift of tongues.

Let's for a moment go back to Acts chapter two, and see what type of language was given that day. Acts 2:5-11, *"And there were dwelling at Jerusalem Jews, devout men, out of every nation under heaven. Now when this was noised abroad, the multitude came together, and were confounded, because that every man heard them speak in his own language. And they were all amazed and marvelled, saying one to another, Behold, are not all these which speak Galilaeans? And how hear we every man in our own tongue, wherein we were born? Parthians, and Medes, and Elamites, and the dwellers in Mesopotamia, and in Judaea, and Cappadocia, in Pontus, and Asia, Phrygia, and Pamphylia, in Egypt, and in the parts of Libya about Cyrene, and strangers of Rome, Jews and proselytes, Cretes and Arabians, we do hear them speak in our tongues the wonderful works of God."*

So, when you read the verses in context, it is plain to see the languages the Holy Ghost gave at that event were those of the people who lived there and in other parts of the world. It even mentions the different languages. They were all amazed because some of these disciples, like Peter, were unlearned and would not have known how to speak in those languages. We also see that the tongues were given so that all these people could hear *"the wonderful works of God. "*

Paul admits that not all that are born again have the gift of tongues, *"And God hath set some in the church, first apostles, secondarily prophets, thirdly teachers, after that miracles, then gifts of healings, helps, governments, diversities of tongues. Are all apostles? are all prophets? are all teachers? are all workers of miracles? Have all the gifts of healing? do all speak with tongues? do all interpret? But covet earnestly the best gifts: and yet shew I unto you a more excellent way. "* 1ˢᵗ Corinthians 12:28-31. This, again, would

152

prove that not all believers would be able to do what Jude told us to do.

Now I am not going to debate whether speaking in tongues is Scriptural or not. I personally have not received such a gift even though, at times, I was a part of the charismatic belief where most people believe that a sign of being filled with the Holy Spirit is speaking in tongues. I also have many friends that believe in speaking in tongues and do it themselves. I have seen people who, by their actions, seem to be filled with God, and God seems to have His anointing on them to speak in tongues. It is no problem for me that they speak in tongues. I personally, will stay the way I am unless God shows me differently.

I do know this, if you have been filled with the Holy Spirit, according to Galatians 5:22-23, these things should be flowing out of you, *"But the fruit of the Spirit is love, joy, peace, longsuffering, gentleness, goodness, faith, Meekness, temperance: against such there is no law."* If you don't have those qualities, I don't care how many tongues you speak in; you don't have the filling of the Holy Ghost.

Before we go further in seeing how to pray in the Holy Spirit, let's look at how not to pray. James 4:3 says, *"Ye ask, and receive not, because ye ask amiss, that ye may consume it upon your lusts."* From what is given here, we can get a clue of what Jude might be talking about. When we read what James says, we can see that praying in the Holy Spirit is not praying for our own selfish gains and desires. I fear too many times when we pray to God, it is about us more than others. Like the old saying, "bless me and mine, thee and thine," or "Lord, my name is Jimmie, I'll take all you give me." So, to pray in the Holy Spirit must be the opposite of this type of praying.

It is very important that we find out how to pray in the Holy Spirit because it is part of our defense against Satan and Paul lists it as part of the armor of God, *"And take the helmet of salvation, and the sword of the Spirit, which is the word of God: Praying always with all prayer and supplication in the Spirit, and watching thereunto with all perseverance and supplication for all saints..."* Ephesians 6:17-18.

We also know that the Spirit will pray for us when we don't know how to pray, *"Likewise the Spirit also helpeth our infirmities: for we know not what we should pray for as we ought: but the Spirit itself maketh intercession for us with groanings which cannot be uttered. And he that searcheth the hearts knoweth what is the mind of the Spirit, because he maketh intercession for the saints according to the will of God."* Romans 8:26-27. I thank God that the Spirit does this because I have gone through some trials that broke me and left me without words, drowning in a puddle of tears. But through the Holy Spirit praying for me and His help, I was able to overcome.

I think the one we should turn to to find out how to pray in the Holy Spirit is part of the God-head, Jesus Christ. The disciples asked Christ how to pray, and He answered them, which is recorded in a couple of places. We will draw from Matthew 6:6-13, *"But thou, when thou prayest, enter into thy closet, and when thou hast shut thy door, pray to thy Father which is in secret; and thy Father which seeth in secret shall reward thee openly. But when ye pray, use not vain repetitions, as the heathen do: for they think that they shall be heard for their much speaking. Be not ye therefore like unto them: for your Father knoweth what things ye have need of, before ye ask him. After this manner therefore pray ye: Our Father which art in heaven, Hallowed be thy name. Thy kingdom come, Thy will be done in earth, as it is in heaven. Give us this day our daily bread. And forgive us our debts, as we forgive our debtors. And lead us not into temptation, but deliver us from evil: For thine is the kingdom, and the power, and the glory, for ever. Amen."*

We first notice in the instructions that Christ gave us not to pray so that others can hear what a great speaker you are or how much you can talk. We also find out that God knows what we need even before we ask. I might ask for a million dollars, but God might know that I can't handle that much money. So, instead of giving me the million dollars, He supplies my daily needs. We can see more about that as we briefly summarize the Lord's Prayer.

He starts off, *"Our Father."* Hallelujah!!! He wants us to know that when we are praying, we can pray with authority because the God of all, the one that can do all, supply all, see all, and controls all, is OUR HEAVENLY FATHER! We have a right to enter the throne room of the Most High and make our petitions known because of the adoption that was provided to us by the blood of Jesus Christ. I can cry, ABBA FATHER!!! He is not like an earthly father with limitations. He, unlike an earthly father, never fails. He can protect and guide us so much better because He knows the ending from the beginning and has overcome everything. What an honor to be able to call Him FATHER!!!

Christ goes on to say, *"which art in heaven."* He is situated above everything, and His authority reaches from the highest heavens to the lowest depths of hell. Everything is under his foot. When He decrees something, it is settled, and no one or nothing can stop it. When we properly pray to Him, even the forces of hell can't intervene.

Next, we are to understand that God is holy, *"Hallowed be thy name."* Because of His holiness, we should enter the throne room with respect and reverence, and we should try to enter with our lives as holy as possible. We shouldn't go in with a demanding demeanor but with humbleness and gratitude that we can even attempt to enter.

He goes on to say, *"Thy kingdom come."* His rulership is not just in the heavens but in all the universe. He will one day set up a kingdom here on earth and do away with sin and death, and no army will be able to defeat Him in doing so.

Then we should desire that God's will be done, *"Thy will be done in earth, as it is in heaven."* Our focus should be on God's will instead of our own. That is hard to do. Christ showed the example, however, when He was in the garden. He asked for God to spare Him from drinking the bitter cup, but even though his flesh didn't want to go through with it, He still said, *"not my will but thine be done."*

There is another small word in this statement that, to me, is a huge word: *"in* earth." When God created man, He created him out of the dust of the earth. Once I became a child of God, the Holy Spirit now lives inside this earthly body. I feel this means I should allow God's will to be done "in" my earthly body as He sees fit, not only His Will to be done in all the earth, but in me individually as well.

We see a list of valuable instructions next, *"Give us this day our daily bread. And forgive us our debts, as we forgive our debtors. And lead us not into temptation, but deliver us from evil."* In this, we are to depend on God to supply all of our needs and not worry about tomorrow, knowing that He has it under control. We see that we are to forgive other people if we are to be right with Him. We should be able to do that when we look at how much we need forgiveness from God because of the way we live. We need to ask God to lead us in our walk and give us the power to overcome evil and temptation. We must depend on God to protect us because Satan is out to get us to fall and rob us of our testimony.

Finally, we are to pray that everything that is done by us, and even our prayers, should bring God honor and glory, *"For thine is the kingdom, and the power, and the glory, for ever. Amen."* He alone is worthy of all praise.

So, from what I gather from the way that Christ taught us how to pray, we can understand more about how to pray in the Spirit. To pray in the Spirit, to me, would be 1. Praying using God's Word and authority. 2. Not only praying to God for our needs but also hearing from God to find out what He needs from us. 3. Agreeing with God and allowing the Holy Spirit and Christ to be our intercessors to interpret what would be best for us. 4. Pray that God will place in our hearts such a desire for Him that His desires will also become our desires. 5. Pray that God will fill us with Divine love so that we can love God and man as He loves us. 6. Pray in the authority of Christ and not in our power.

I believe those qualities are what praying in the Spirit is. I should also mention I don't think you can pray with all those attributes if you haven't placed all the other things Jude said to add to your faith in your life and are practicing them. By having God lead us and fill us, we can be assured that we will pray in the Spirit, and because it is aligned with God's Word, He will hear, and He will answer.

So, after building upon our faith all the things that Jude had told us about, he then says in verse twenty-one, *"Keep yourselves in the love of God..."* How can we keep ourselves in the love of God? I will start by using an example that most of you might be able to understand. Do you remember when you met your first love? Everything about them was wonderful. You would fix them something to eat, and they might have had a habit of smacking, but to you, it sounded like sounds of enjoyment of the meal you cooked for them. And the burp that followed was confirmation that they thoroughly enjoyed your cooking.

Then you might want to take them out to a concert or some other event, and they are late getting dressed every time you do. You would look at them when they finally came out and say, "Seeing how beautiful you are now was well worth the wait."

When you talked on the phone, you would talk for hours upon hours. Neither one wanted to be the first to hang up, so you would say back and forth to each other, *"you hang up, no you hang up, no you hang up."*

158

OH! And the statement that love is blind is more accurate than most people believe. I have seen women that could be a model going out with Billy Bob, who had very few teeth, was skinny as a rail, always had dirty fingers and clothes, and had absolutely no class. They would be the type of person that people used to say was one that *"Only a mother could love."* But yet, she would think he was prince charming. That goes for the opposite sex, too, because I have dated some of those.

So what makes a person overlook all of those faults of the person they are dating? Because they are in LOVE! That being said, if they stay together long enough, that LOVE will be tested, and if they are not careful, all those habits that were so adorable will become, to the person that loves them, a nightmare.

I, in the past, have dated some beautiful women who could be a model only to find out they had an awful attitude. I don't care how beautiful you are; if your attitude is terrible, it won't be long before you are ugly to me. People who saw us together would say, *"You are one lucky dude."* I would think, "Would you like to take her off my hand?!"

Fortunately, God's love for us is so great that we are ALWAYS precious in His sight. His love is everlasting and unconditional. But as with any strong relationship, that relationship can be hindered if you don't spend enough time with each other. With God, His love won't change, but with us, if we start spending less time with Him, our love will begin to go after other things to occupy our time. Our relationship with God will then suffer.

If we want to keep a good relationship with God and stay in that perfect love with Him, we must take the time to listen to what He has to say. We must spend quality time with Him in His Word and our prayer life. We must do all we can to please Him and be obedient to what He has told us to do. I know this sounds one-sided for a relationship, but it is not; God always does His part for us. The Bible says in John 14:15, *"If ye love me, keep my commandments."* And by obeying this, He has promised in John 15:10 that we will stay strong in love, *"If ye keep my commandments, ye shall abide in my love; even as I have kept my Father's commandments, and abide in his love."*

So, what do we get out of our obedience and following Him? Glad you asked because when we do that, we are in the position to be *"...looking for the mercy of our Lord Jesus Christ unto eternal life."* Jude verse 21. We are firm in a relationship with Him because of the love that God had already given us through His Son, Jesus Christ. And that is vitally important.

Why? Because we were once enemies of God. *"For if, when we were enemies, we were reconciled to God by the death of his Son, much more, being reconciled, we shall be saved by his life. And not only so, but we also joy in God through our Lord Jesus Christ, by whom we have now received the atonement. Wherefore, as by one man sin entered into the world, and death by sin; and so death passed upon all men, for that all have sinned:"* Romans 5:10-12.

God loved mankind so much in the beginning that He made Him a place where mankind would never have to worry about sickness, weather, animals, provisions, or even death. All man had to do was obey one little commandment, to not eat of the fruit of the tree of "the tree of knowledge of Good and Evil," and man couldn't even keep that part of the bargain.

God, being holy and unable to look upon sin, would have to judge sin. He didn't want His creation, the one that He longed to have fellowship with and to love, to disobey and bring that judgment on himself. But man, greedy for position, authority, selfish desires, and pride, succumbed to rebelling against God to get what he wanted.

The moment man did that, he found himself under the curse that God warned him about before eating the fruit. He was now an enemy of God sentenced to both a physical death from this world and a spiritual death from God forever. *"But God commendeth his love toward us, in that, while we were yet sinners, Christ died for us."* Romans 5:8.

God's love for us was so great that even though He had provided everything that man would ever need and want, and man rejected that love and His gifts, He gave up His own Son to restore His relationship with man. Because of that love and mercy, we don't have to be enemies of God. We don't have to face the wrath that is to come. By trusting in Christ's atonement, we can now look for mercy to everlasting life rather than judgment to everlasting death! It is only through that mercy that we can know with confidence that we will be with God throughout eternity, once again in a position to have everything we could ever imagine and more than the mind can contain.

I want to emphasize that it is all because of God's mercy. Although we may have built up our faith, prayed in the Holy Ghost, and kept ourselves in God's love, all those things cannot merit Heaven. After all the diligence, earnestness, self-denial, watching, and obedience that we can muster, we must still look for the MERCY of the Lord Jesus Christ to bring us to eternal life. And because of His mercy, we can now do as Titus 2:13 says, *"Looking for that blessed hope, and the glorious appearing of the great God and our Saviour Jesus Christ."*

"Behold, what manner of love the Father hath bestowed upon us, that we should be called the sons of God..." 1st John 3:1. As you can see now, it is not a one-sided relationship that you are in with God; he has given and continues to provide far more than what He expects in return.

If we are now in the position of walking in the love of God and filled with His Spirit, the things that burden God should burden us. Therefore, we need to strive to stay in that position and not let the world or others remove us from it. If we are not watchful and careful, Satan will send distractions or one of his servants to speak something wrong in our ear, and we will find ourselves again outside the will of God.

I pray to God that both you and I stay strong in the faith. In shame, I have fallen in the past, failed, and walked away because of hurt from church people and believing the lie that Satan gave me. But praise God, by His mercy, I was able to get back on track.

When we walk in the Spirit, the Bible tells us that we shouldn't rejoice when one falls away, but we should have compassion and mercy and try to convince them to return to the faith. We are also commanded to compel the lost to come to God. But these are two different things and need to be treated as such. We must listen to God on how and what to say to each individual. There is no blanket statement we can give to everyone we contact. People have different emotions and reactions to what people say to them.

I remember my dad saying he almost didn't accept Christ as his Savior, and the reason might shock you. Dad had lost his father figure when he was only in the 5th grade, and he then had to go to work to help supply for the family. He said that many would come to him trying to get him to trust God as His father. That was the wrong thing to say to dad because when he thought of a father figure, he thought of one that had almost beaten him to death on two occasions and would have had his mother not intervened. His father figure was nothing to want, and as a matter of fact, dad didn't even go to his funeral and said, "I'm glad the old "blank" is dead."

Another example I can give is my sister. When we were younger, we were a part of a denomination that believed you almost had to be perfect to go to Heaven. If you truly know the Word of God, you know that is impossible to do in the flesh. My sister said she would try so hard to be holy, but every time she slipped up, she felt like such a failure. She felt God was not pleased with her, and no matter how much she tried, she would never be able to do all that was required to be holy. So one day, she finally decided if she couldn't do it, why bother and pretty much gave up, losing all hope that she would ever be good enough. I have felt that way many times in my life, and maybe you have. Once again, thank God for His mercy that will sustain us and help us walk a better life. No, we won't ever be holy, but we can strive to be, and what we lack, Christ's blood is more than sufficient for the rest. These two different things that had happened with two different people require two different approaches to reaching them.

For this reason, Jude writes, *"And of some have compassion, making a difference."* Jude verse 22. The *"difference"* is between people that have fallen and those that are just hard and profane. The people that Jude is referring to here are people who have begun to doubt their faith. They are not just downright evil, but maybe because of their lack of a faithful walk or because of some event that has happened in their life it has caused them not to trust God. Or maybe, it could be from some false teacher that has convinced them of another way.

These types of people need to be drawn in with compassion and mercy. They have been hurt enough and don't need some super saint to tell them how awful they are and will never be worthy. They could be the type of people that may take a long time to bring back into the fold because of their hurt, maybe even from some of the body of Christ. We need to be with them as Christ is for us, kind and longsuffering. We need to treat them with kindness and gentleness, not in a self-righteous way. We always need to remember, *"but by the grace of God, there go I."*

164

Then some people are set deep in their sinful condition, and they seem not to care that they could die and be in eternal damnation at any moment. They have totally turned their backs on God. God spoke of that type in Amos 4:11, "I have overthrown some of you, as God overthrew Sodom and Gomorrah, and ye were as a firebrand plucked out of the burning: yet have ye not returned unto me, saith the LORD."

Jude moves on to say, *"And others save with fear, pulling them out of the fire..."* Jude verse 23. These people are heading to hell because of a sin debt, but they don't have to be. Romans 6:23 says, *"For the wages of sin is death; but the gift of God is eternal life through Jesus Christ our Lord."* It is the job of the believer to try and lead these people to the Lord, and we need to warn them in vivid detail of their pending doom. Paul says in 2nd Corinthians 5:11, *"Knowing therefore the terror of the Lord, we persuade men; but we are made manifest unto God; and I trust also are made manifest in your consciences."*

However, when we confront these people, we must do it in love. Paul gives us instructions on this as well, in 2nd Timothy 2:24-26, *"And the servant of the Lord must not strive; but be gentle unto all men, apt to teach, patient, In meekness instructing those that oppose themselves; if God peradventure will give them repentance to the acknowledging of the truth; And that they may recover themselves out of the snare of the devil, who are taken captive by him at his will."*

Many times when we witness to these types of people, they often get angry and don't want to talk about it. But still, yet, we need to warn them. It is not an easy task at times, but there is a Scripture in the Bible that might give us more determination and zeal to obey God when He moves on our heart to talk to someone about their salvation, *"When I say unto the wicked, Thou shalt surely die; and thou givest him not warning, nor speakest to warn the wicked from his wicked way, to save his life; the same wicked man shall die in his iniquity; but his blood will I require at thine hand."* Ezekiel 3:18. I, for one, don't want to be standing watching a person be dragged to hell while they yell back at me, "But you didn't warn me! You knew the truth. You were already saved and secure. Why would you not warn me?"

Hell is such an awful place that even people in hell want to warn people not to go there. In Luke chapter 16, we are given an account of a man that found himself in hell. Many take this as a parable that Jesus was telling. However, the personal name of the beggar was given, which leaves me to believe this to be an actual event.

The story starts in Luke 16:22 and continues until the end of the chapter. I am going to include the whole story in the book because some of you reading it may be lost and have never heard details about hell.

> *"And it came to pass, that the beggar died, and was carried by the angels into Abraham's bosom: the rich man also died, and was buried; And in hell he lift up his eyes, being in torments, and seeth Abraham afar off, and Lazarus in his bosom. And he cried and said, Father Abraham, have mercy on me, and send*

166

*Lazarus, that he may dip the tip of his finger in water,
and cool my tongue; for I am tormented in this flame.
But Abraham said, Son, remember that thou in thy
lifetime receivedst thy good things, and likewise
Lazarus evil things: but now he is comforted, and
thou art tormented. And beside all this, between us
and you there is a great gulf fixed: so that they which
would pass from hence to you cannot; neither can
they pass to us, that would come from thence. Then
he said, I pray thee therefore, father, that thou
wouldest send him to my father's house: For I have
five brethren; that he may testify unto them, lest they
also come into this place of torment. Abraham saith
unto him, They have Moses and the prophets; let
them hear them. And he said, Nay, father Abraham:
but if one went unto them from the dead, they will
repent. And he said unto him, If they hear not Moses
and the prophets, neither will they be persuaded,
though one rose from the dead."*

There are a few things I would like to take away from the
story of Luke. First, from the description of hell, it is a place
that no one would want to go to, much less spend eternity.
Secondly, the man had a choice of going or repenting and
not going, but once he was there, there was no way out.
Thirdly, the rich man had compassion (something he didn't
have while on earth) and wanted to warn his family not to
come to where he was because it was so bad. Finally, notice
that Abraham admitted that people who are stooped in their
sin so far are hard to convince to repent.

My friend, if you haven't trusted the Lord, you must get
that settled before you die. Man doesn't know when that day

appointed for him is, so I would not tarry concerning your salvation. Once death comes, you will be where you have chosen to be without hope of changing your situation.

Then in the last part of verse 23 in Jude, it says, *"hating even the garment spotted by the flesh."* There are a few opinions on exactly what this means; one of those concerns is the garment itself. Garments in the Bible sometimes have a particular meaning. For instance, a purple robe stands for royalty and represents the King of Kings, Jesus Christ. Another is scarlet, which points to the blood atonement that Christ paid for our sin. Revelation talks about people receiving a white or fine linen robe which points to not only the Righteous One, but also those to whom He has imputed His righteousness because of their faith in Him.

Here, the garment appears to have been stained by the smoke of sin. Sin, to the believer, should be disgusting and repulsive. The garment here can be compared to the filthy rags used by lepers to cover their decaying bodies. When a person had leprosy, their body would rot, and parts of the body, like fingers and toes, would eventually fall off. They would wrap the infected areas that oozed with putrefying pus, and once the rag was saturated, they would discard it. These rags had a disgusting smell. Sin should be viewed with the same attitude; it leaves behind a stench that only Christ can cure.

When a person had leprosy, they had to stay away from others to avoid spreading the disease. This brings us to the other interpretation. Many believe that the verse means that Christians should avoid being around the sinner's behavior for fear it may infect them. Some people think that if they get into a relationship where the person is not saved, they can win them to the Lord. But most of the time, the opposite happens. We should shun sin and avoid all situations that could cause temptation.

I want to mention that even though we should hate sin and avoid it as much as possible, we still need to love the sinner. Christ going to the woman of Samaria proves this. The holier-than-thou Jews wouldn't go near Samaria because they were considered sinners, on the same level as dogs. Jesus knew it wasn't the people themselves, but sin that dwelled on the inside as a result of man's fall in the garden. We are no better than anyone else, and Jesus doesn't condone that kind of behavior of self-righteousness. Only through Christ are we worthy to be children of God.

But no matter how you view the verse, we definitely need to stay away from all means of temptation. 1st Thessalonians 5:22 warns, *"Abstain from all appearance of evil."* Satan is smart and cunning, and our bodies in the flesh are bent to sin. Therefore, we should keep a watchful eye, stay prayed up, and read up to help give us strength when facing temptation but avoid it as much as possible. In the Lord's prayer, He even mentions to *"Lead us not into temptation."* Man in his sinful condition is weak, but we can be overcomers through Christ and the power of the Holy Spirit. Keep your garments CLEAN.

Jude now begins to conclude his letter. *"Now unto him that is able to keep you from falling..."* Jude verse 24. I think that is the best start to end with after all the negative actions of

169

some of the people in the church that Jude went over. With all the warnings and judgment, we find that there is still hope and that hope is in Christ. It is through Him and Him alone that we will be able to fight against the enemy.

Look at just a glimpse of how He will keep us. *"I will lift up mine eyes unto the hills, from whence cometh my help. My help cometh from the Lord, which made heaven and earth. He will not suffer thy foot to be moved: he that keepeth thee will not slumber. Behold, he that keepeth Israel shall neither slumber nor sleep. The Lord is thy keeper: the Lord is thy shade upon thy right hand. The sun shall not smite thee by day, nor the moon by night. The Lord shall preserve thee from all evil: he shall preserve thy soul. The Lord shall preserve thy going out and thy coming in from this time forth, and even for evermore."* Psalms 121. *"Fear thou not; for I am with thee: be not dismayed; for I am thy God: I will strengthen thee; yea, I will help thee; yea, I will uphold thee with the right hand of my righteousness."* Isaiah 41:10. We find these types of protection for the saint all throughout the Bible. He truly is able!

Not only is He able to keep us from falling, but he adds, *"and to present you faultless before the presence of his glory..."* 1st Thessalonians 5:23, *"And the very God of peace sanctify you wholly; and I pray God your whole spirit and soul and body be preserved blameless unto the coming of our Lord Jesus Christ."* It is because of the completed work of Christ. God views us through the holy, perfect, and sinless blood of His Son.

170

1ˢᵗ Thessalonians 3:13, *"To the end he may stablish your hearts unblameable in holiness before God, even our Father, at the coming of our Lord Jesus Christ with all his saints."* Colossians 1:22, *"In the body of his flesh through death, to present you holy and unblameable and unreproveable in his sight."* No wonder we will see Him face to face *"with exceeding joy!"* We are redeemed by the Blood of the Lamb!

Again, we owe it all *"To the only wise God our Saviour..."* Jude verse 25. *"What can wash away my sins, nothing but the blood of Jesus? What can make me whole again? Nothing but the Blood of Jesus."* To Him *"be glory and majesty, dominion and power, both now and ever. Amen."* As the old Dottie Rambo song says, *" Nothing good have I done to deserve God's own Son. I'm not worthy of the scars in His hands. Yet He chose the road to Calvary to die in my stead. Why He loved me, I can't understand."* All Praise to His holy name!

Chapter 12

Apostasy in the Church Today

When we look at America and the nations of the world, there is no doubt in my mind that we are living in the last days. As I had mentioned, God never sends wrath without warning us first. Luke 17:26-27 states, *"And as it was in the days of Noe, so shall it be also in the days of the Son of man. They did eat, they drank, they married wives, they were given in marriage, until the day that Noe entered into the ark, and the flood came, and destroyed them all."*

If we look at the above verses, we can tell that we are in that setting where Noah was. If that is true, just like in Noah's day when the wrath of God was poured on mankind, we are about to see the wrath of God fall on this world in the near future. Peter and Jude both warned about what to look for; Peter recalled the flood and Jude, Sodom, and Gomorrah as examples.

I will give you just a few examples of where we are in the depravity of man today. In the beginning, God created male and female. That was, and for the record still is, all the genders that we have. Yet, in today's society, man has developed over 81 types of genders and gender identities. Just because you say you are a lion doesn't make you a lion. If identifying yourself as something makes you what you say you are, then I identify myself as physically fit and rich, neither of which is the case.

They have created these false identities so they can live out the sinful lust in their lives. If you are unsure of what identity you are, let me help you find out. Stand in front of the mirror naked. If you see a male anatomy part, you are a male; if you don't, you are a female. That is basic biology, and I will not charge you for my professional diagnosis.

This mindset of gender identity is mostly prevalent among young people. Unfortunately, we are helping this kind of thinking along with the curriculums taught in our school systems. Children as young as eight years old are being taught about oral and anal sex as well as transgenderism.

I thought nothing would shock me anymore in my life until I read an article in the Dailywire about a superintendent of a California school defending a 7th-grade boy masturbating in front of his classmates. He even called it normal, I quote, "I don't think any of you would want us up here chatting about an issue that took place with your child," said McLaughlin. "I would say that, at least once a year, this comes up from both males and females within a school setting. And so, I don't think this is anything outside the norm."

What a twisted and sick era we live in! But where is the true blame? Number one, people like the superintendent above need to be fired, and the school curriculums to leave sex education of young people to the parents, not the school system. Secondly, parents need to take on the responsibility of training their children and stop leaving it up to someone else. The Bible says in Proverbs 22:6, *"Train up a child in the way he should go: and when he is old, he will not depart from it."* The sad thing is, even if a parent does want to train their child correctly, the government will often deem the

173

parent unfit to parent because they see them as intolerant or a threat to society for instilling in them moral values.

One of the problems is, however, parents today don't seem to have a moral compass enough to guide a child. Add to that, many children today learn about sex because of their parent's involvement in porn. The porn industry makes it so readily available on the internet and seems to target young people's sites that children often visit. How many times have you opened a legit site only to be redirected or bombarded by pornography and pornographic images?

It seems every moral and godly behavior in our country is under attack. They are trying to go as far as labeling Christians along with terrorist groups. They obviously don't know what true Christianity is, because it is not hate; it is all about love and concern for our fellow man. The Ten Commandments have been taken out of public and judicial systems, and prayer has been taken out of schools. Churches are being attacked because of fundamental doctrine.

They treat the church differently than the world. During the Covid 19 pandemic, many places, including bars, were allowed to stay open while churches had to shut their doors. When churches were finally allowed to meet, they had to do so under very strict rules, although professional sports didn't have to live by the same standard. Even though living by the guidelines, some churches were given hefty fines. Because of this, along with many members being afraid to come back, many churches had to close their doors.

Our nation has sanctioned same-sex marriages, set "gay pride month" into place, and even lit up the White House with the gay flag colors to show solidarity with the group in the last days Obama's term. I remember when people tried to hide their sins; now, it's out in the open. The Bible said that one day, even women wouldn't blush about their sins anymore. Jeremiah 6:15, *"Were they ashamed when they had committed abomination? nay, they were not at all ashamed, neither could they blush: therefore they shall fall among them that fall: at the time that I visit them they shall be cast down, saith the LORD."* Sadly, this behavior is in the local church today.

Under the protection of abortion on demand, our nation kills over 14 million babies by chemical abortions each year. On June 4, 2019, there was a bill called the H. R. 5 Act, which they said would protect people's sexual orientation. That bill is being revised in 2022 to expand its definition. If successful, it will open the door to the government having the right to shut down churches that preach against homosexuality or any other sexual behavior. It could give the right for a pedophile to do what they do because it is a part of their sexual orientation, and it would deem any speech against these kinds of sexual actions as hate talk, which would give them the authority to lock up the offender. Our government has become intolerant of the gospel but yet calls the church intolerant to others.

Our government is causing division now. Black against whites, republicans versus democrats, conservatives versus liberals, Christians against non-believers, vaccinated and not vaccinated. They are brainwashing the public to trust science, but remember, Hitler used science to make his

175

people believe the Jews should be killed. It is God whom this nation was set up to trust, **not man, not science**. America has been a strong and wealthy nation, but we will face extreme judgment because she has turned her back on God.

Even though these signs point toward the coming judgment, Jude is not talking about the external forces that might be against the church. He is talking about the internal teachings of the church. Again, apostasy, by definition, is the abandonment of a religious or political belief. In Jude, he is talking about the church moving away from what God's Word said. We keep blaming it on our government and outside people, but in reality, we are allowing the church to defeat the church.

Although Jude doesn't give full details about what the false teachers were teaching during his time, we can, however, by looking between the lines, see some things that we can grasp to help us better understand what to look for.

First, when we look at their doctrine, we see they didn't understand what grace was and were denying Jesus Christ. They trusted in their own knowledge and understanding rather than God's revelation and guidance, and they didn't understand the working of the Holy Ghost.

We know in their practice, we see that they were licentious. They would corrupt and pervert teachings and butter up people for their own personal gains. They rebelled against Divine and civil authority. They lived by whatever felt good, "just do it," instead of God's principles, even at the cost of defiling themselves. They are self-centered and prideful.

In their identity, we see they are a part of the Christian community. It appears that these people are probably both Jews and Gentiles. These same types of actions are in our churches today. As Jude did then, we need to warn our youth, families, and friends because of the evil coming into our churches.

About 75% practice Buddhism, Christianity, Hinduism, Islam, and Judaism today. Out of that number, the top two are Islam, with 1.6 billion people, and Christianity, with 2.17 billion. That sounds like a lot of people, and Christianity is prospering; however, if non-believers were a religion, it would be the third largest group with 1.13 billion people. The church has a long way to go.

Here are some more statistics on the church. 80% believe pastoral ministry has negatively affected their families. Many pastors' children do not attend church now because of what the church has done to their parents. 66% of church members expect a minister and family to live at a higher moral standard than themselves.

The moral values of some Christians are no different than those who consider themselves non-Christians. The average American will tell 23 lies a day. 34% of pastors wrestle with the temptation of pornography or visit pornographic sites. 57% of pastors feel fulfilled but yet discouraged, stressed, and fatigued. 84% of pastors desire to have close fellowship with someone they can trust and confide in. The profession of "pastor" is near the bottom of a survey of the most-respected professions, just above "car salesman.".

Many denominations are reporting an "Empty Pulpit Crisis." It is not a shortage of ministers but a shortage of ministers desiring to fill the role of a pastor. 45% of American adults say they attend religious services, an all-time low. This information is quoted and found at https:..www.pastoralcareinc.com/statistics/.

According to Lifeway, in 2021, six out of ten churches are plateaued or declining in attendance. More than half of their churches saw fewer than ten people who became Christians in the last 12 months. And Barna reports that 38% of pastors are thinking of quitting the ministry, 51% from mainline denominations. The church is not in a good position today.

To show how much our churches have begun to turn away from the truth of God's Word, I will give you some examples of churches that I knew of personally in the Atlanta area and the practices that were going on. Some of you may know these people as well. I want to say that I am not trying to put them down or expose their dirty laundry. Some of these I still consider my friends. But, the Christian believer must expose false doctrine and teachings. I am also using them instead of many others I could use because their story has already been told nationally through interviews and news media from which I have obtained this information.

One of these so-called Pastors/Bishops is Jim Swilley, who named his church correctly enough. It was called, "The Church in the Now." According to sources, this individual married a woman even though he and she knew he was gay. They were married for 21 years. His wife was even a co-pastor there in their mega-church. His wife encouraged him to admit his sexual orientation of being gay, which would better show the church's motto: *"Real People Experiencing the Real God in the Real World."*

Here is a quote from him after coming out about being gay, *"**I have favor with God** and man, and the positives in my life so far outweigh the negatives, that I can't **think of myself** as anything but **blessed**, I am surrounded by love, even in the midst of some expected persecution."* Although he knew that being gay was an abomination, he tried to justify his stand by giving the Scriptures, which condemned other things that were abominable to God. Two wrongs don't make a right!

To his defense, there are many. A list of just a few is in Proverbs 6:16-19, *"These six things doth the LORD hate: yea, seven are an abomination unto him: A proud look, a lying tongue, and hands that shed innocent blood, An heart that deviseth wicked imaginations, feet that be swift in running to mischief, A false witness that speaketh lies, and he that soweth discord among brethren."* He, using some of these abominations, further stated, *"I could go on, but, suffice it to say, we are probably all guilty of regularly committing abominations (ever had a 'proud look' on your face, or eaten a pork chop?), so we need to keep the use of that word in perspective," "Thank God for the Lamb of God who took away the sin of the world!"*

Let me quote what two well-known preachers said about Jim Swilley's book entitled, "20/20 Vision: Changing Your Life by Changing the Way You See Things." The late Bishop Eddie Long, whom I had admired at the start but not after his true identity came out, stated about the book, "In a way that only he can, Bishop Jim **Swilley has taken the principles of Scripture and made them practical and**

179

doable. 20/20 VISION challenges its readers **to elevate their perception from being down-trodden, victimized, and hopeless to being empowered, capable, and victorious.**"

Another well know television preacher, Dr. Mark J. Chironna, said, "My friend, Bishop Jim Swilley, has written this **masterpiece**…and it is a sure invitation to **a larger life by making that fundamental shift in your perception of reality.** If you ever doubted whether God had more in store for you, this book **will change your paradigm forever.** Let the words of this book **give you the permission you need to open the windows of your perception,** change the way **you view yourself and the world you live,** and watch both you and that world undergo an **incredible and remarkable transformation.**"

My friend, trying to justify your sin because others have sinned also will not work when it comes to God's holiness and what he expects us to do. And for the record, when you are practicing a deliberate sin you are committing, YOU DO NOT HAVE FAVOR WITH GOD!

You will also notice many other popular false preachers say that they are "blessed and highly favored" and try to convince their audience they are, no matter their lifestyle. That, my friend, is a LIE straight from the pit of hell!

After divorcing his wife, Jim Swilley eventually married his husband, Ken Marshall. Swilley now pastors a congregation called Metron, which meets at Landmark Midtown Art Cinema, or at least at the time of the report. Here is his quote, *"Being married as yourself, preaching as yourself, and living your life as yourself is infinitely better*

180

than doing those things as someone else." Believe it or not, they all still have a rather large following of so-called Christians. And for the record, we are not supposed to live our lives to ourselves; we are to live as unto the Lord.

Here is a tweet from Debye Swilleys' tweeter account, "Deb Swill…Certified Life Coach (coming soon), **iconoclast**, center for **empowerment**, worldwide **motivator**, and Rockin **Love Goddess** Guru! Woop!" She was at that time co-pastor of the Chruch in the Now, along with her husband and gay husband. In her appearances, you probably will never hear about Jesus or traditional doctrine as she speaks more on being spiritually **enlightened** vessels, how we are all an extension of the universe and of creation, we all have a "**divine spark**," and God dwells in everyone. It is the basic "**universal faith**" message that is being spread, which is not the gospel but a cult formed by the Devil himself to destroy the church.

There is an old saying, "An apple doesn't fall far from the tree," which is true in this case. Jim Swilley is the nephew of the late "Bishop" Earl Paulk. Bishop Paulk pastored the Cathedral of the Holy Spirit in the Atlanta area. The church grew to 12,000 members and was one of the first to welcome gay and lesbian members openly.

I believe that gays and lesbians should be able to attend church. That is the best way to hear God's Word and be led by the Spirit to be saved. However, no one, gay, bi, straight, or whatever, according to the Bible, should be allowed to become a member when they live an open, rebellious, and sinful lifestyle. It scars the body of Christ and gives a poor testimony to the transforming power of the Holy Spirit.

They speak to the congregation, telling them they must have some spiritual authority over them; interestingly enough, they have no one over them. As a matter of fact, long ago, the family left the Church of God that was over them so they could start their own church and allegedly also because of an admitted adulterous affair. Once again, this is according to news articles and people who claim to have known the situation.

The affairs didn't stop there; they continued while he was pastor of the Cathedral of the Holy Spirit. One of the affairs was with Mona Brewer, which he admitted to, but said Mona was the initiator. WHAT? You expect me to say it is okay that this church leader had sex because a woman tempted him first?!

To make things worse, on October 14, 2007, Donnie Earl Paulk admitted that he thought all of the 34 years he lived with Don Paulk, Bishop Earl Paulk's brother, that he was Don Paulk's son, only to find out that a paternity test revealed his real father was Earl Paulk. His mother said she had the relationship with Earl Paulk not as a sexual encounter but to carry on Don Earl's name since her body was killing Don Earl's sperm.

Other allegations included women from the old Church of God saying that not only had Bishop Earl Paulk had sexual relations with them, but also Don Paulk and two other nephews who were ministers at the church, and some of the women claimed they were only seven years old when it started. According to one accuser, she was told she was doing the will of the Lord in serving her pastor in that capacity.

After the scandal and the megachurch folding, Donnie Earl eventually started a church as well. Unfortunately, even though he has, up to this point, as far as I know, never had a problem with accusations about illicit affairs, the message he preaches is just as wrong. It is called "The Gospel of Inclusion."

He believes that God doesn't exclude any religion, including Wiccans, gays, and lesbians, and that God accepts them all. To one point, I agree God does open the door to salvation to everyone, but He does not condone or accept anything that differs from His Word or anyone who tries to make it to Him without His Son, Jesus Christ.

Donnie Earl further doesn't believe there is a hell except for the one people create with their own actions. He doesn't believe that people need a man of God to teach them truths because God is inside them (another scripture that has been taken out of context). Here are a couple of direct quotes from Donnie Earl, "It's not just live and let live," It's God in all of these streams. That thing you call Jesus. The thing you call the Prophet Mohammed they call Buddha. It's just different names, but it's the same spirit."

He probably derived that way of thought from Bishop Carlton Pearson, who supported Bishop Earl Paulk after his fall. Carlton Pearson, a well-known mega pastor, also lost his megachurch for preaching a message of universal salvation: God doesn't just accept Christians but people of other faiths. He, too, didn't believe in a literal hell.

In Donnie Earl's church, according to interviews of people who have attended, you can find all types, Gays, agnostics, Muslims, and even a Wiccan priest at one time. On the walls of the church, you can see pictures of Mahatma Gandhi and Rev. Marin Luther King Jr. on the walls.

According to the reports, if you look at the window over the pulpit, you can see a Christian cross with symbols from Islam, Judaism, and Hinduism around it. In the middle, you will see a dove, which to them, symbolizes the spirit of peace that binds all religions and people together.

This is nothing more than the modern co-exist belief of today. A former member of Chapel Hill, part of the Earl Paulk legacy, described Donnie Earl's ministry perfectly. She said the bishop twisted Scripture to prey on people for riches, glory, and lust. Donnie Earl, in her view, is just another manipulative pulpit predator.

One of the family's so-called preachers came to one of the churches that I attended. I was both shocked and appalled when in a mixed audience of men and women, boys and girls, he began to teach how masturbation wasn't only accepted by God but was good for you!

The church I was attending was yet another large one from this family lineage. It amazes me how much of this family's heritage had large churches, and some still have. I saw many things about how this church was run that weren't right with God's teachings.

Every one of the family's churches I attended made you call the leader bishop; many warned you would face the judgment of God if you spoke against them, and some, even if you left the church. They deceived their members into believing they were the voice of God.

I far as I can remember, as long as I was at the church, I heard not one sermon on salvation or that the only way to God was through His Son, Jesus Christ. But believe me, I heard tons of messages on how God would bless you if you gave to the church and you need to understand that the "Bishop" is the word of God.

Just by the examples I have given here; you can see almost all of the things Jude warned about are found in these churches. I wish I could say that this group of churches was the only one teaching their people these false teachings, but there are many, and it has been happening for years. As a side note, I want to mention that I still love the people I mentioned earlier and pray that they will come to know the truth one day.

To give another example of the depravity of some churches, my uncle, who was a preacher, told of a church that he had heard of in North Carolina that would turn off all the lights and let the members grope and make out with each other. They believed this was a part of "brotherly love." Can you imagine what God thinks?

When I started a small church in Florida, I came across a well-known local televangelist. He had many followers and preached prosperity. His main song all of his people would sing along with him was, "I looked into your future, and your future looks better than it does right now. Right now. Right now. Right now, right now, right now."

He visited my church and later contacted me with a proposition. He told me that if I assured him he would make $3000 per month, he would invite me to his broadcast regularly and even come to speak at my church free of charge. I replied with a simple note that said, "Thanks but no thanks!"

That prosperity message and the wolves that come to devour the flock and deceive them by twisting the Scriptures have been around for a long time in America. I remember "Reverend Ike" with his famous quotes like, "I don't want to wait for my piece of the pie in the sky by and by; I want mine now with whip cream on it." And "You can't lose with the stuff I use."

He and many others on television promised that if you sent them money, God would miraculously bless you so much you would be rich. Their message contained only concepts of material satisfaction and self-motivated prosperity, but the only problem was they were the only ones getting rich.

Once I was shocked to find out Heaven was running out of money, or so this man made it seem. It was Oral Roberts; he told the television audience that God would end his life if he didn't raise one million dollars by a specific date. I thought, my Lord, does he really expect people to believe Heaven is broken and God is a crook holding someone hostage for ransom?

186

These people prey on the weak, just like the wolves in sheep's clothing the Bible speaks of. People with cancer, they say, can be healed if you buy their cloth that was put in the Jordon river, or God will stop that foreclosure if you send them money.

The list of these false television evangelists that prey on people goes on, from Jim and the late Tammy Faye Bakker, Joel Osteen, the late Robert Schuller, and Paula White, to name a few, all of which are either trying to get your money or convince you that there is no standard that God sets for people in their lives nor hell that must be faced if turning from God and His standards. Many of these and others have terrific sins they are covering up in the closet, but one day God will reveal them, if not in this world, in the judgment to come.

I also want to share with you some statements that I found from others according to the Lamb & Lion Ministries article, "Apostasy in the Church." According to this article, the Episcopal Bishop of New Jersey, John Spong, denies the virgin birth, the miracles of Jesus, the resurrection, and the second coming and believes that Paul and Timothy were homosexual lovers.

While in an interview with Phil Donahue, Norman Vincent Peale stated, "It's not necessary to be born-again. You have your way to God; I have mine. I found eternal peace in a Shinto shrine... I've been to Shinto shrines, and God is everywhere."

Also, in an interview with Phil Donahue, the late Robert Schuller, a well-known television preacher, was quoted as saying, "The Cross sanctifies the ego trip. That's very significant. In other words, Jesus had an ego. He said, "I, if 'I' be lifted up, 'I' will draw all men to 'me.' Wow! What an ego trip He was on!"

He had further made this statement; "I don't think anything has been done in the name of Christ and under the banner of Christianity that has proven more destructive to human personality and, hence, counterproductive to the evangelism enterprise than the often crude, uncouth, and unchristian strategy of attempting to make people aware of their lost and sinful condition."

As an independent Baptist, I was most shocked at a statement from R. Kirby Godsey, the president of Mercer University, which the Georgia Baptist Convention heavily supported at that time. He denied, among other things, the infallibility of the Bible, the unique power and authority of God, the validity of the gospels' account of the life and teaching of Jesus, the efficacy of Christ's atonement, and the uniqueness of Christ as the only Savior.

Most of these examples are from the past but let me mention a summary of what is going on today. You can find gatherings over the internet and in local churches where they are now trying to justify sinful and even satanic worship as Christian. Titles like "Christian witches," "Christian Wicca," "Christian mediums," "Christian psychics," and now "Christian yoga." They use catchy phrases that appeal to the flesh and pride, such as higher consciousness and the use of crystals, spirit channeling, and psychic powers.

Many are called inter-faith denominations, not inter-denomination. What is the difference? Inter-faith can include any or all of the above; inter-denominations are people of at least the traditional faith in Christ Jesus coming together.

Another modern trend is called, The "seeker-friendly church." They do studies in the community to see what people want and then conform the church to their desires instead of what God's Word says. Some of these even have open sex in the church itself.

My friend, this is like gender identity, only Christian identity. Just because you put Christian in a title doesn't make it a Christian activity or church doctrine. For instance, with "Christian witches mediums, psychics and Wicca," you can't mix satan and his works with God.

And "Christian yoga?!" How do you think a practice like yoga, a Hindu practice where even the postures are a vital part of sorcery, and false religion bent to change your mental and spiritual thinking, be Christian? Yoga is not inviting Jesus in; it is inviting the "Kundalini" spirit in. The two can't exist in the same body. You, again, can only serve one master, God or the devil. We can't just all get along, 1st John 3:10 says, *"In this the children of God are manifest, and the children of the devil: whosoever doeth not righteousness is not of God, neither he that loveth not his brother."*

And again, we were warned they would come. 1st Timothy 4:1 states, *"Now the Spirit speaketh expressly, that in the latter times some shall depart from the faith, giving heed to seducing spirits, and doctrines of devils; Speaking lies in hypocrisy; having their conscience seared with a hot iron…"* and 2nd Corinthians says, *"For such are false apostles, deceitful workers, transforming themselves into the apostles of Christ. And no marvel; for Satan himself is transformed*

189

into an angel of light. Therefore it is no great thing if his ministers also be transformed as the ministers of righteousness; whose end shall be according to their works."

Let me remind you again what Isaiah said in chapter 5:20-24, *"Woe unto them that call evil good, and good evil; that put darkness for light, and light for darkness; that put bitter for sweet, and sweet for bitter! Woe unto them that are wise in their own eyes, and prudent in their own sight! Woe unto them that are mighty to drink wine, and men of strength to mingle strong drink: Which justify the wicked for reward, and take away the righteousness of the righteous from him! Therefore as the fire devoureth the stubble, and the flame consumeth the chaff, so their root shall be as rottenness, and their blossom shall go up as dust: because they have cast away the law of the LORD of hosts, and despised the word of the Holy One of Israel."*

The word "woe" in these verses is a term of judgment. It is the term used to pronounce that something bad is coming for the person it is addressed to. It means that judgment will come for them either in this life or possibly the final judgment spoken of in the book of Revelation.

The Bible tells us about these people and what to do when we come across them; 2nd Timothy 3:2-7, *"For men shall be lovers of their own selves, covetous, boasters, proud, blasphemers, disobedient to parents, unthankful, unholy, Without natural affection, trucebreakers, false accusers, incontinent, fierce, despisers of those that are good, Traitors, heady, highminded, lovers of pleasures more than lovers of God; Having a form of godliness, but denying the power* *thereof: **from such turn away**. For of this sort are they which creep into houses, and lead captive silly women laden with sins, led away with divers lusts, Ever learning, and never able to come to the knowledge of the truth. "*

People, as the Bible warned, are looking for a church that will make them feel good about themselves. They don't want condemnation or correction. They are looking for a church to say it's okay to drink, smoke, have illicit affairs, have a gay lifestyle, or whatever, and yet still be able to call themselves a Christian.

So why do people run to these types of false teachers? The answer is in 2nd Timothy 4:3-4. "For the time will come when they will not endure sound doctrine; but after their own lusts shall they heap to themselves teachers, having itching ears; And they shall turn away their ears from the truth, and shall be turned unto fables."

Paul goes on to say, *"Because that, when they knew God, they glorified him not as God, neither were thankful; but became vain in their imaginations, and their foolish heart was darkened. Professing themselves to be wise, they became fools, And changed the glory of the uncorruptible God into an image made like to corruptible man, and to birds, and fourfooted beasts, and creeping things. Wherefore God also gave them up to uncleanness through the lusts of their own hearts, to dishonour their own bodies between themselves: Who changed the truth of God into a lie, and worshipped and served the creature more than the Creator, who is blessed for ever. Amen. "* Romans 1:21-25.

Man's sinful nature doesn't like to be told what to do. God is a gentleman; He will not force Himself on anyone. You

191

have free will to do as you please, but if you rebel against God, your heart will darken, and you will begin to not know the difference between good and evil and soon face the judgment of that behavior.

Romans 1:28-32 further explains the consequences of your willfulness of turning away from God, *"And even as they did not like to retain God in their knowledge, God gave them over to a reprobate mind, to do those things which are not convenient; Being filled with all unrighteousness, fornication, wickedness, covetousness, maliciousness; full of envy, murder, debate, deceit, malignity; whisperers, Backbiters, haters of God, despiteful, proud, boasters, inventors of evil things, disobedient to parents, Without understanding, covenant breakers, without natural affection, implacable, unmerciful: Who knowing the judgment of God, that they which commit such things are worthy of death, not only do the same, but have pleasure in them that do them."*

Galatians 6:7-8 says, *"Be not deceived; God is not mocked: for whatsoever a man soweth, that shall he also reap. For he that soweth to his flesh shall of the flesh reap corruption; but he that soweth to the Spirit shall of the Spirit reap life everlasting."* Contrary to what these false teachers say, you can not live any way you please and be blessed and highly favored. You will bring trouble into your life as well as the judgment of God.

God tells His children, *"Beloved, believe not every spirit, but try the spirits whether they are of God: because many false prophets are gone out into the world. Hereby know ye the Spirit of God: Every spirit that confesseth that Jesus Christ is come in the flesh is of God: And every spirit that confesseth not that Jesus Christ is come in the flesh is not of*

192

God: and this is that spirit of antichrist, whereof ye have heard that it should come; and even now already is it in the world." 1st John 4:1-3. We need to read and understand God's Word, line upon line, precept upon precept.

Paul warns, *"But though we, or an angel from heaven, preach any other gospel unto you than that which we have preached unto you, let him be accursed. As we said before, so say I now again, If any man preach any other gospel unto you than that ye have received, let him be accursed."* Galatians 1:8-9.

And just what is that gospel that has been preached? Paul defies these false teachers' claim that all religions lead to God. He shows what the true gospel is about, *"Moreover, brethren, I declare unto you the gospel which I preached unto you, which also ye have received, and wherein ye stand; By which also ye are saved, if ye keep in memory what I preached unto you, unless ye have believed in vain. For I delivered unto you first of all that which I also received, how that Christ died for our sins according to the scriptures; And that he was buried, and that he rose again the third day according to the scriptures: And that he was seen of Cephas, then of the twelve: After that, he was seen of above five hundred brethren at once; of whom the greater part remain unto this present, but some are fallen asleep. After that, he was seen of James; then of all the apostles. And last of all he was seen of me also, as of one born out of due time."* 1st Corinthians 15:1-8. *"For there is one God, and one mediator between God and men, the man Christ Jesus; Who gave himself a ransom for all, to be testified in due time."* 1st Timothy 2:5-6.

Peter expounds on it more by saying in Acts 4:12, *"Neither is there salvation in any other: for there is none other name under heaven given among men, whereby we must be saved."* The full gospel is Christ coming in the flesh, living a sinless life, dying on the cross, rising from the dead, and ascending to heaven to make the atonement of sin. Only through Him can a person be saved, not Buddha, Mohammed, or even your works; it's all in the name of Jesus Christ!

The Bible tells us in Proverbs 3:7, *"Be not wise in thine own eyes: fear the LORD, and depart from evil."* The Bible also warns that we should be concerned about God and His will, *" And fear not them which kill the body, but are not able to kill the soul: but rather fear him which is able to destroy both soul and body in hell."* Matthew 10:28.

As Jude warned the church, here is some warning in the Scripture I want to give concerning the church today. 1st Peter 5:8, *"Be sober, be vigilant; because your adversary the devil, as a roaring lion, walketh about, seeking whom he may devour..."*

Ephesians 5:3, *"But fornication, and all uncleanness, or covetousness, let it not be once named among you, as becometh saints..."* and verse eleven, *"And have no fellowship with the unfruitful works of darkness, but rather reprove them."*

In closing, let me give you some more modern things to prove the church is in apostasy today. Did you know that some Christian-based Bible publishers are printing gender-neutral Bibles because of pressure from our society? The United Church of Christ in the year 2000 even set up a

$500,000 scholarship fund dedicated to gay and lesbian seminarians. Over 48% of congregations are now allowing an openly gay or lesbian couple to be full-fledged members. But even worse, over 26% of them allow gays or lesbians to assume lay leadership positions.

Even more shocking, almost 70% of so-called Christians don't agree that Jesus is the only way to God, and out of the 80% of people in America that believe in God, only 56% of those believe the God they put their trust in is the same God in our Bible. My Christian brothers and sisters, it is time to wake up!

It is up to the true born-again believers to teach the world and warn them about these false doctrines. Christ, Himself told us, *"...All power is given unto me in heaven and in earth. Go ye therefore, and teach all nations, baptizing them in the name of the Father, and of the Son, and of the Holy Ghost: Teaching them to observe all things whatsoever I have commanded you: and, lo, I am with you alway, even unto the end of the world. Amen."* Matthew 28:18b-20.

We need to walk the life of a Christian, and we need to correct and, if need be, put away those in the church that are causing divisions or teaching false doctrines. WE NEED TO BE SANCTIFIED AND WALK IN THE POWER OF THE HOLY SPIRIT!

I have tried to use as many Scriptures as possible to show the truth in God's Word, and many I have repeated because they bear repeating. I have also mentioned judgments coming very often. Please take heed of those warnings.

With all the false teaching out there, I would be remiss if I didn't take the time to ask you a very personal question. Do you know Jesus Christ as your personal Savior? Have you ever asked Him into your life and repented of your sin? If not, I want to give you some Scriptures that can help you have a new life in Christ Jesus.

Did you know that you can know for sure that you are going to Heaven when you die? To do so, you must realize all of mankind are sinners. *"For all have sinned, and come short of the glory of God"* Romans 3:23. This would include you!

Did you know that there must be a price paid for sin and that payment is death? Romans 6:*23, "For the wages of sin is death; but the gift of God is eternal life through Jesus Christ our Lord."* That is the price that all of mankind owed. Because of the sin debt in your own personal life, you should pay the debt with your very life.

Did you know that there is a way where you don't have to give your life to pay the sin debt that YOU owe? Romans 5:8, *"But God commendeth his love toward us, in that, while we were yet sinners, Christ died for us."* Christ died for YOUR Sin debt, but there is something you must do for that payment to be accepted.

You must agree with God that you are a sinner and in need of a Savior. You must be sorrowful for the condition you are in. You must agree that there is nothing in your power to be able to pay for the sin debt that you owe. You must ask for Jesus to come into your life and to repent (turn away) from your sinful lifestyle. God will give you the power to do that.

196

It's not hard to do. It is as simple as this prayer. Will you say it with me? *"Dear Lord Jesus. I know that I am a sinner. Please forgive me and come into my heart and save me right now. I know I am not worthy of this payment, but you have offered it, and right now, I am accepting that payment for myself. Thank you, Lord, for saving my soul and taking me in as your child. I will do my best to live for you from this day forward."*

If you said that prayer from your heart and truly meant it, you are now a born-again Christian. In Romans 10:13, the Bible says, *"For whosoever shall call upon the name of the Lord shall be saved."* God promises that He will save you if you call on Him. I want to be the first to welcome you into the family of God.

The next thing you need to do is find a good, Bible-believing church so that you can grow in your new Christian faith. If you don't know where to go, contact us at www.treeoflifecoaching.org, and we will try our best to find you a good church in your area.

The Bible tells us, *"But the hour cometh, and now is, when the true worshippers shall **worship** the Father **in spirit** and **in truth**: for the Father seeketh such to worship him. God is a Spirit: and they that worship him must worship him **in spirit and in truth**."* John 4:23-24.

In order to understand in today's messed up world what the true spirit and truth are, we, as believers of Jesus Christ, need to *"Study to shew thyself approved unto God, a workman that needeth not to be ashamed, rightly dividing the word of truth."* 2nd Timothy 2:15. We need to avoid the snare that satan is spreading and stay firm in our doctrine and salvation so that we can be that beacon of light to lead others to the TRUTH during these last days of modern-day apostasy.

Thank you for reading this book. I hope it has not only been a blessing, but a challenge to keep up the fight for the faith.

For your convenience, I have left a couple of pages for you to put in your personal notes.

May God Bless you on your spiritual journey.

To learn more about Roger Bilbrey, to purchase more of his books, or to contact him, please visit:

www.treeoflifecoaching.org

NOTES